WALKER'S COMPANION

IRELAND

WALKER'S COMPANION

IRELAND

DAVID HERMAN
Photography by Michael J. Stead

BROCKHAMPTON PRESS

ACKNOWLEDGEMENTS

I would like to thank the following most sincerely for their generous help in researching and editing this book. Any remaining errors in content are of course my own responsibility.

To Dawson Stelfox for information on Cecil Newman; to Graham Seymour and James McEvoy of the Northern Ireland Department of the Environment for details of right-of-way legislation in Northern Ireland; to Jimmy Murphy of Cospoir for information on Long Distance Routes; to Paddy Prendergast of the Ordnance Survey and Maurice Sheehy of Ventry for information on the tracks of Mount Eagle; to Sylvia and Victor Morrow who calmed my rising panic when faced with the Beenkeragh Ridge (it didn't turn out to be so terrifying!); and to Mark Herman who edited the 'semi-final' manuscript.

Last (and primarily) to my wife Mairin Geraty who pondered nearly every word in the manuscript and who walked nearly every mile of the routes with me.

This edition published 1999 by Brockhampton Press,
a member of the Hodder Headline PLC Group.

ISBN 1 86019 8791

First published in 1995 by Ward Lock

Text © David Herman 1995
Photographs © Ward Lock 1995

This book is based on material originally published in the *Great Walks* series.

Printed in Dubai by Oriental Press

CONTENTS

INTRODUCTION TO THE ROUTE DESCRIPTIONS

1. ACCESS   See page 124.
              NB The representation in this book of a road, track or path is not evidence of the existence of a right-of-way.

2. ASCENT   The amount of climbing involved in each route has been estimated from the appropriate map and should be regarded as approximate only.

3. CAR-PARKS   Many routes start at a public car-park. For other routes places are indicated where a car can be parked by the wayside, but it must be done with care, as indiscriminate parking can be a great nuisance to local people.

4. INTERESTING FEATURES   The best position for seeing these is indicated both in the route descriptions and on the maps by *(1)*, *(2)*, etc.

5. LENGTH   These are strictly 'map miles' estimated from the appropriate map; no attempt has been made to take into account any ascent or descent involved.

6. MAPS   The maps are drawn to a scale of approximately 1:25 000 or 1:50 000 and all names are as given on Ordnance Survey maps. Field boundaries in particular, which can be a mixture of hedge, fence and wall, should be taken as a 'best description'. The arrow on each map points to grid north. The scale of some small features has been slightly exaggerated for clarity.

   A discrepancy has arisen between the OS imperial and metric maps. Mathematically-inclined readers armed with a calculator and much idle curiosity will have noticed that the imperial heights given in this book do not always correspond to the metric. The reason is that the heights are taken from the relevant metric and imperial maps and these do not exactly correspond, either because they are recorded on slightly different points or because of the higher accuracy of the metric.

SYMBOLS USED ON ROUTE MAPS

□	Ruin	△	Summit
X	Gate	⧸⧹	Cliff
⊣⊢	Bridge		
⊣⊢	Waterfall		
·····	No path		
---	Path		
===	Track		
+++	Fence		
■	Occupied building		
⊤⊤	Stile		
∞∞	Wall		
▲	OS Obelisk		
✠	Church		

The letters 'L' and 'R' stand for left and right respectively. Where these are used for changes of direction they imply a turn of about 90° when facing in the direction of the walk. 'Half L' and 'half R' indicate a half-turn, i.e. approximately 45°.

7. ROUTE DESCRIPTION

The briefest examination of the route descriptions that follow will show that the routes described cover an enormous range of both length and difficulty; the easiest can probably be undertaken by a family party at almost any time of the year whilst the hardest are only really suitable for experienced walkers who are both fit and well-equipped. Any walker therefore who is contemplating following a route should make sure before starting that it is within his or her ability.

It is not easy in practice, however, to give an accurate picture of the difficulty of any route, because it is dependent upon a number of factors and will in any case vary considerably from day to day with the weather. Any consideration of weather conditions must, of course, be left to the walker himself (but read the

8. STANDARD OF THE ROUTES

section on safety first). Apart from that, it is probably best to attempt an overall assessment of difficulty based upon the length, amount of ascent and descent, problems of route-finding and finally, upon the roughness of the terrain.

Each of the routes has therefore been given a grading based upon a consideration of these factors and represented by the bold numerals which precede each walk title. A general description of each grade follows:

Easy (1) Generally short walks (up to 5 miles, 8 km) usually over well-defined paths, with few problems of route-finding. Some climbing may be involved, but mostly over fairly gradual slopes with only short sections of more difficult ground.

Moderate (2) Rather longer walks (averaging about 8 miles, 13 km), but with sections where route-finding will be more difficult. Mountain summits may be reached with climbing over steeper and rougher ground.

More strenuous (3) Generally longer walks (averaging about 10 miles, 16 km), with prolonged spells of climbing. Some rough ground calling for good route-finding ability, perhaps with stretches of scrambling.

Very strenuous (4) Only for the few, involving long distances (up to 15 miles, 24 km), with a considerable amount of climbing, and perhaps stretches of scrambling.

The walks are arranged in order of increasing difficulty within each region. A summary of each walk is given at the beginning of each route description with information on length, amount of climbing and any special difficulties, such as scrambling, that will be met along the way.

9. STARTING AND FINISHING POINTS The location of each starting and finishing point is described along with its six-figure grid reference (see page 125).

10. TIME FOR COMPLETION The usual method of estimating the length of time needed for a walk is by Naismith's Rule: 'For ordinary walking allow one hour for every 3 miles (5 km) and add one hour for every 2000 feet (600 m) of ascent; for backpacking with a heavy load allow one hour for every $2\frac{1}{2}$ miles (4 km) and one hour for every 1500 feet (450 m) of ascent.' However, for many this tends to be over-optimistic and it is better for each walker to form an assessment of his or her own performance over one or two walks. Naismith's Rule also makes no allowance for rest or food stops or for the influence of weather conditions.

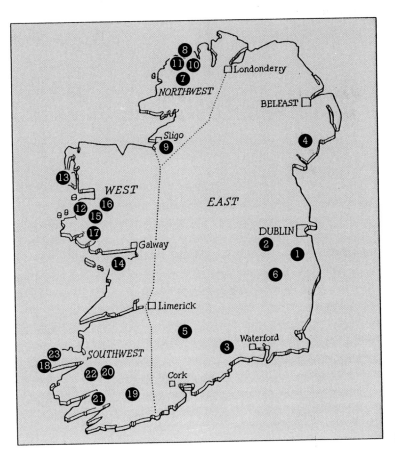

Route locations

In Northern Ireland there should be no difficulty with road designations. The system used is identical to that used in the rest of the United Kingdom; that is, A, B and C designations. In the Republic of Ireland, however, an older system — T (for trunk) and L (for link) — is gradually being replaced by N (for national) and R (for regional) not necessarily respectively. While the changeover of the main roads to N is virtually complete, many secondary roads still have the old T or L designation. Worse still, some signposts indicate T or L and others R. For this reason, both designations have been used in the text where appropriate.

Many minor side-roads have no designations and may even be too modest to demand signposts. Nevertheless, they must be negotiated to reach the start of some of the walks in this book. To minimize the chance of getting lost in this confusing network, *precise* distances (to tenths of a mile or km) have been given, rather than the usual rougher approximations, where necessary. In these instances, it would be prudent to measure distances using the car's odometer. It is rather a nuisance, but better than the frustration of getting lost in a maze of minor roads.

11. GETTING TO THE STARTING POINT BY CAR

Introduction

Even a casual glance at the map of Ireland on page 9 will reveal that the East covers a large area, the whole island except the Atlantic seaboard, and that it contains a number of high mountain ranges, most of them in the south of the region. These ranges are not quite as wild and rugged as those further west, and they are surrounded by 'civilized' farmland, with towns and even cities close by, rather than by the inhospitable barren land of the west. Nor is the sea all that much in evidence; and when seen it is tame and placid. Access to these mountains by car, as might be expected, is comparatively easy though it is certainly not effortless, as some of the complicated access directions will testify.

In this large and diverse area, two routes, or rather two mountains, stand out: the two Munros. Galtymore in the Galtees can be reached by a very easy but dull route from the south or a somewhat longer and much more attractive route encircling high corries on the northern side — an easy choice. Lugnaquillia in Wicklow can be climbed by several good routes. The circuit of the Glen of Imaal, the route to Lugnaquillia finally chosen, is strenuous, but the long, lingering high-level descent from the summit offers fine panoramic views.

The Glen of Imaal is on the quieter, western side of Wicklow (quieter, that is, when the Artillery Range in Imaal is not in use). The two other routes in Wicklow are on the sharper eastern side, the side of steep glacial valleys and corries etched into otherwise rounded mountains. The Cloghoge Valley is the loveliest in Wicklow, a superb blend of woodland, valley and lake, and a good area for visitors who have only a short time to spend around Dublin. This whole area is now safe in the arms of the new Wicklow National Park, a most welcome development.

One cautionary and sad word on Wicklow before moving on. Do not leave valuables visible in your car; better, do not take valuables with you at all into any area of the Wicklow Mountains, remote or not. There have been too many cases of robbery in this region to risk it.

Between the Galtees and Wicklow lie the Comeraghs, probably the finest mountains in the area between these two major

ranges. They are noted for their dramatic corries (and are notorious for their dull bleak uplands), one of which is probably
rightly reputed to be the most dramatic corrie in Ireland. This
has not been included in a route, because the route chosen, with
three fine corries, gives better overall variety.

Glendalough, the mine workings

Far to the north in County Down are the Mournes, a small but
rugged range of uneroded granite mountains, and with Connemara by far the best-mapped area in the entire island. The route
included here is a short but steep ascent to castellated Slieve
Bearnagh.

Lastly there is Robertstown, an area where the nearest hills
are but a faint blue smudge on the eastern horizon. Its quiet
backwaters, under-used canals and out-of-the-way villages are
just the place to recuperate after the rigours of the mountains.

1·1

THE CLOGHOGE VALLEY

STARTING AND
FINISHING POINT
On the L of the
R759/L161 heading
towards Sally Gap
(172064). Take the
R755/T61 and turn
west (R coming
from Dublin) onto
the R759. Drive
uphill for 2 miles
(3.2 km) and park
near the pillars on
the L.

MAPS
OS 1:50 000 Sheet
56 and OS Wick-
low District 1 inch
to the mile.

LENGTH
4 miles (6.5 km) for
the easy route; 6
miles (9.5 km) for
the harder.

ASCENT
700 ft (210 m) for
the easy route;
1700 ft (520 m) for
the harder.

NOTE FOR
DOG-OWNERS
The longer route
runs through a
deer-rearing area
and the land is
poisoned.

Wicklow at its most scenic, a complex interplay of woodland and valley, lake and mountain, which is reminiscent of the less rugged, more scenic parts of England's Lake District. Two routes are described and both give marvellous views of Lough Tay, the rocky cliffs of Luggala which end in great boulders at its lakeshore and the partly wooded Cloghoge Valley (pronounced '*Clock-oge*') which connects Tay to Lough Dan, the large secluded lake to the south. The *easy* route works its way diagonally down to the floor of the Cloghoge Valley and returns on a short but sharp ascent from near the shores of Lough Dan to attain a higher level than on the outward stretch. The *harder* route diverges from the easy one near Lough Dan, continues along the north shore of the lake, climbs rocky Knocknacloghoge and returns through a side valley to the road.

ROUTE DESCRIPTION (Map 1.1)

Go through the gates labelled 'Ballinrush' 70 yards (65 m) down-hill from the large pillars and on the same side *(1)*. The walk from here to Lough Dan is as navigationally simple as it is scenically delightful: a straightforward stroll along a track downhill or level almost all the way *(2)*. (You will realize that there is an unpleasant snag to a looped walk which starts innocently with a lot of downhill.) When private property in the form of a large forbidding gate blocks the way ahead turn R down a narrow path through an ancient wood to the bank of the Cloghoge River directly opposite a two-storey house — a lovely place for a bite to eat and a rest. The two routes part ways here.

Easy route Return along the path to the main track. Turn L onto it and branch first R steeply uphill onto a green track just before the first holiday home. At the first ruin on the L, turn R again steeply uphill with forest on the R. Turn L at the first track (it plunges on the R into forest) and follow it across open country, which gives marvellous views L across to the high peaks of the range.

When forest blocks the way ahead, turn R uphill on another track thus heading for a prominent gate on the skyline. Pass through it, turn L and with forest on the L continue straight ahead through forest. Where a forest road sweeps in — and away — on the R, cross the fence L and follow the track all the way back to the road. Turn L and walk the few yards back to the starting point.

Harder route Wade across the river using a rough weir a little way down-stream of the two-storey house. Turn L and pick up a path which hugs the northern shore of Lough Dan. At the spit of

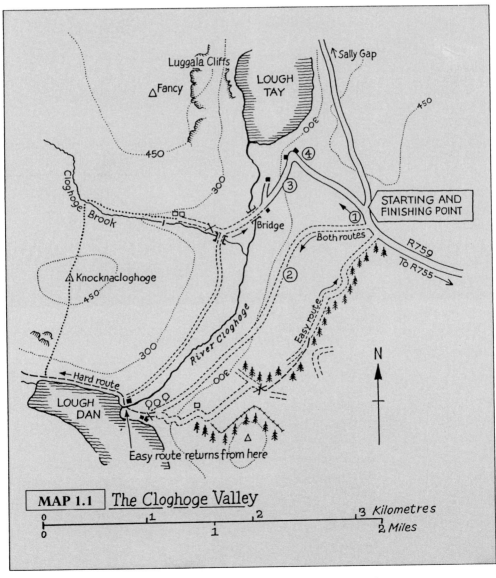

MAP 1.1 The Cloghoge Valley

Lough Tay and Luggala cliffs

silver sand, which marks the western end of the lough turn R steeply uphill avoiding the crags L on the climb. At the sudden easing of the slope, head for the L of the two rocky hillocks ahead, picking up a path that improves as it nears the summit of Knockacloghoge (1754 ft/534 m).

From the summit walk directly north over rough, heathery ground to cross the Cloghoge Brook, then turn R downstream following the L-hand bank closely. At a delightful pool below a tiny waterfall, join a green track and follow it through a gate and thence down to a main track. Turn L here, cross a wide bridge and walk to tarmac at a farmhouse on the R. Continue uphill *(3)* to a hairpin bend *(4)* and beyond it take the steep incline to the road and the starting point.

The Cloghoge Valley and Lough Dan

1   *The Peregrine Falcon*

The peregrine falcon nests on the Luggala cliffs which can be seen from the start, but better from the end of the walk. A fast and strong flyer, it has fast wing-beats interrupted by occasional gliding. Its wing span is about 3 ft (0.9 m). The bird is rare in Ireland (and elsewhere) but its range is slowly spreading.

2   *Heather*

The heather moorlands here are a blaze of purple in August, when walking across them produces a cloud of pollen. This area is generally reputed to be the best-managed heather moorland in Wicklow.

3   *Luggala House*

The elegant house which is built on the northern shore of Lough Tay, but only whose grounds are visible on this steep ascent, is owned by a member of the Guinness family (of brewing fame). Many famous people have visited the house, including the philosopher Bertrand Russell, who was captivated by the scenery. He returned years later and could not find the spots from which he had previously so enjoyed the view. He concluded philosophically that one should not re-visit places which one enjoyed the first time round.

4   *Two Irish Miles*

A notice on the house on the L encouragingly (and a trifle whimsically) announces in archaic Irish lettering and in plain English that it is 2 Irish miles to Lough Dan. It does not say that an Irish mile is considerably longer than an English one. The distance is actually 2 *standard* miles because the notice exaggerates the Irish mileage — so we are back to square one! At this juncture you will probably be less concerned about that and more about the climb to the road and the car. For the record, the climb is 300 (English) ft (90 m).

1·2

Canals of Kildare

Kildare is a flat inland county, and one not normally associated with walking. Nonetheless a system of walking routes has been laid out using as a centrepiece the canals that run through the county on their way from Dublin to the west and south-east. These routes traverse a country of pleasant villages and wet fields bounded by straggling unkempt hedges. Much of their length follows shallow, rarely used canals, arched by high humped-back bridges, whose banks support wildfowl, dragonflies and a variety of flowers. If you find that canal banks are a trifle tedious, take heart; the first stretch of canal bank is followed by sections of country road, forest and bog-land, which should refresh you before the final length of bank.

Route Description (Map 1.2)

Following the gaudy signpost of the Kildare Way, cross the prominent Binn's Bridge in Robertstown *(1)* to reach the north side of the canal, thus leaving the main part of the village. Take the road beyond, continuing straight ahead along a narrow road beside the canal where the main road swings R. Just before Lowtown Marina, cross Fenton Bridge, pass around the Marina buildings *(2)* and cross the high footbridge beyond, where a signpost announces far-off and exotic destinations culminating in St Mullins 70 miles (112 km) away.

Turn L beyond the footbridge and walk along the towpath, passing one road-bridge (do *not* cross it). At the second bridge continue straight ahead onto a metalled road, pass Ballyteige Castle *(3)* and a lock; just beyond it, turn R onto a side-road, thus following the purple arrows of the 'Robertstown Local Walk' (you follow these to the end of the walk).

Take this narrow road, further on a rough farm road, initially through an area of scattered houses and later through a state forest, and past turfworkers' billets on the R *(4)* (both forest and billets appear by their unkempt and desolate appearances to be reverting to the gentle care of nature). Pass a turn on the L and at

STARTING AND FINISHING POINT
Robertstown, County Kildare (790249). The village is situated 2 miles (3 km) south of the R403/L2.

MAPS
The OS half-inch to the mile Sheet 16 covers the area and should be useful for the route to Robertstown, but is on so small scale that it is of marginal use on the walk. A leaflet with a sketch-map covering all the Kildare canal walks is available from Cospoir – see Appendix.

LENGTH
8 miles (14 km)

ASCENT
Negligible.

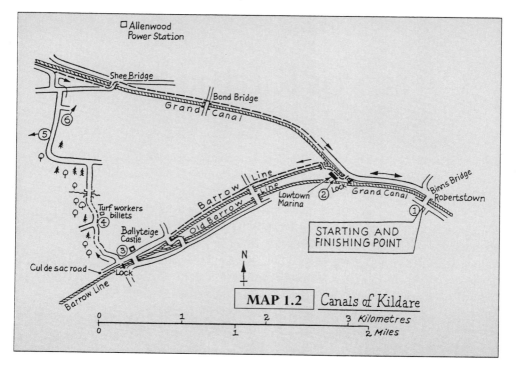

MAP 1.2 | Canals of Kildare

a T-junction turn L to pass to the R of the end of a raised bog (5), with the cooling tower of Allenwood Power Station (6) ahead. At the next T-junction turn L onto the main road (not R as instinct for home would rightly suggest), and a few steps along turn R up a side-road, so reaching yet another stretch of canal. Turn R here to follow the towpath to the next bridge, Shee Bridge. Cross this bridge and continue along an overgrown towpath (now on the L bank) past Bond Bridge (do *not* cross this one), so reaching again the canal bank opposite Lowtown Marina. Return along the same side-road as the outward journey to reach Robertstown, turning R over Binn's Bridge to reach the village.

1   Robertstown

The village owes its origin to the Grand Canal, work on which commenced in the middle of the eighteenth century. The large, imposing building in the village was originally a hotel owned by the Grand Canal Company.

2   Lowtown Marina

Lowtown lies at the junction of the Grand Canal and the Barrow Line, so canals radiate from here to Dublin, the River Shannon to the west, and the River Barrow to the south. From Lowtown water levels are controlled and the necessary paperwork to operate the canal is issued.

Opposite: *The bridge at Robertstown*

Lock on Grand canal

3   *Ballyteige Castle*
This is a typical example of an Irish fortified house of the fourteenth to sixteenth centuries.

4   *Turfworkers' Billets*
These were built during the fuel crisis of the 'Emergency', as World War II is still euphemistically called. They were intended as accommodation for workers harvesting peat from nearby bogs, but were never completed.

5   *Lullymore Bog*
On the L is Lullymore Bog, a typical midlands raised bog, and part of what was the Great Bog of Allen before it succumbed to the cutting machinery for nearby peat-burning power stations. Its dome shape is caused by the accumulation of sphagnum, which is able to draw up water so that the bog surface can rise above the water-table.

6   *Allenwood Power Station*
This power station burns sod peat from nearby bogs, Ireland being one of the very few countries in the world to have this type of fuel. The station is still open, having been given a reprieve from closure in the late 1980s.

2·3

CORRIES OF THE COMERAGHS

The central section of the Comeraghs (pronounced '*Come-err-ahs*'), between the Sgilloge Gap and Coumfea 3 miles (5 km) to the south-west, is a dull, boggy plateau which greatly contrasts with the virtual ring of fine corries surrounding it. This walk takes in three of the corries, holding in all six lakes and several small lochans. Each corrie is backed by grassy slopes about 700 ft (210 m) high, here and there broken by protruding horizontal sandstone, while higher up the otherwise smooth skyline is disrupted by an occasional jagged pinnacle. In a surprisingly remote area this is a walk of constantly changing vistas and sudden revelations, with lakes cupped in deep hollows unexpectedly coming into view over heathery hillocks and rolling moorland.

ROUTE DESCRIPTION (Map 2.3)

With the farmhouse on your left walk along the road to the T-junction. Turn R and cross through a gate on the L 150 yards (135 m) along (a truly enormous flat boulder will be visible in the field beyond it). Walk downhill diagonally R towards the river (the Nier, pronounced and sometimes spelt *Nire*) and follow it upstream, crossing what appears to be a major tributary at a clump of trees, but is in fact the Nier itself. Continue straight ahead (thus *not* following the Nier) along an intermittent path beside the stream to walk to the R of a ruin that lies beyond the junction of two more tributaries. The trick here is to pick the correct tributary among the complex gathering of tributaries on the bleak moorland hereabouts: you may need to take a compass-bearing south-east on the lower Sgilloge Lough in order to find it. Walk on the R bank and note, for reassurance, the fence running parallel to the stream on the other bank.

A path develops along the bank of this tributary, and where the fence swings R across the path, look out R for the lower Sgilloge Lough, the least impressive of all the lakes on this route. Continue on a path along the near shore over hummocky ground to the upper Sgilloge Lough (*1*), which is surrounded by a great

STARTING AND FINISHING POINT
In the townland of Lyre (264126). Take the R671/T27 (Dungarvan to Clonmel road) turning onto a minor road opposite Melody's Pub in Ballymacarbry village. Drive straight ahead for 2.1 miles (3.4 km), turning R uphill here. Turn L at an offset crossroads after another 0.5 miles (0.8 km), continue straight on past a R turn, the first on this stretch of road, after another 2.4 miles (3.8 km) and park considerably near a farmhouse on the L after another 0.3 miles (0.5 km).

MAP
OS 1:50 000 Sheet 75

LENGTH
6½ miles (10.5 km)

ASCENT
1500 ft (460 m)

21

amphitheatre cut out of the cliffs with a narrow stream cascading down into its south-eastern corner — a good place for a rest.

The rule from here to the next corrie is to follow the contour of the hillside with the cliffs and high ground close on the L. At the upper Sgilloge Lough swing to the R to walk along the shore. Then walk to the so-far unvisited south side of the lower Sgilloge Lough and continue round the high, grassy ground on the L into the dull moorland at the lower edge of the next corrie, that holding Coumalocha *(2)*. Once into the arms of the corrie swing R away from the cliffs to visit the lower lake, and then walk along the shore to the next lake, which is very close by. This is the

The River Nier

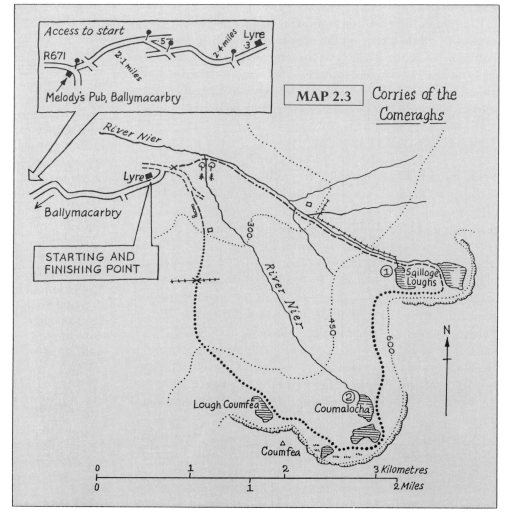

more impressive, though both are lovely. Walk from here over steep little heathery hummocks to the third lake in this corrie, the one nestling under the north-facing cliffs. This lake is backed by an evil-looking swamp that has been fenced in, presumably to keep sheep out.

Continue along the foot of the cliffs to Lough Coumfea, passing on the way the formidable pyramid of the mountain, also called Coumfea (2340 ft/713 m), soaring skyward and so much more impressive from below than on top. Walk the length of the lake on its R-hand side and continue north-west and north along a broad ridge towards fields on a bulge ahead. Before this bulge, cross a gate in a fence and then descend gradually towards the river R (it is the Nier again), keeping well above the thickly vegetated banks. Look out along here for the ruins of an old stone shelter 200 yards (180 m) from the near bank. From this shelter walk parallel to the river, following a path to a corner of wall. Take a track from here downhill (still parallel to the river), continuing straight ahead where it joins a farm road coming in from the R. Follow this round the hill L and back to the start.

1 *Corries*

Corries, the deep hollows gouged out of the sides of the mountains, are a notable feature left from the Ice Age, and this is a good example of one. They were formed as the climate worsened at the onset of the cold. Snow gathered in north- and east-facing hollows sheltered from the prevailing winds and the sun. The snow solidified and accumulated over the years, eventually hollowing out a cliff-rimmed bed. Later still the solidified snow began to creep downhill, forming a glacier, to join other glaciers on the lower ground.

The hummocky ground below the corries on this route are moraines, rough unsorted rubble left behind by the snout of a glacier on its retreat at the end of an ice age.

2 *The Dark Fisherman of Coumalocha*

Even though it is said to be haunted, fishermen are not afraid to spend the night at this lake. The spectre arises from the lake in the dead of night, takes the rod from fishermen who have caught no fish, catches trout for them and returns silently to the depths. This kindly ghost is called the Dark Fisherman of Coumalocha. If you are fishing, it is advisable not to rely entirely on him.

2·4

SLIEVE BEARNAGH

Though the initial walk becomes a little tedious with long views precluded by an increasingly narrow slabby-sided glen, the first, sudden glimpse into the Silent Valley and across to the great arc of peaks around it makes the effort seem trivial. Slieve Bearnagh is the high point, literally and metaphorically, the sets of huge boulders on its summit adding a touch of the spectacular to an already impressive scene. The subsequent views, over the Meelmores and down by Fofanny Reservoir, are more gentle. The walk ends as it began on the Ulster Way. An easy introductory walk to the best of the Mournes.

ROUTE DESCRIPTION (Map 2.4)

Turn L out of the car-park *(1)*, pass the house on the L, and cross the gate L just beyond it to follow the Ulster Way *(2)*. Continue straight through another gate, thus leaving the Ulster Way, and walk up a wide track, ignoring R and L turns which lead to quarry workings *(3)*.

The Hare's Gap between Bearnagh and Slievenaglogh is the first target, and before it the track becomes not so much intermittent as indecisive, spreading heedlessly over a wide area, so that the gate at the gap in the Mourne Wall *(4)* ahead is a useful landmark. At the gap cross this gate *(5)*, so revealing the splendours of the Silent Valley and the high peaks of the Mournes beyond it.

Beyond the gate, turn immediately R to follow the Mourne Wall or, failing that, keep close to the steep slabs where the wall is not continuous. Climb to the two sets of gigantic piles of granite crowning the summit of Slieve Bearnagh (2425 ft/739 m), the first of which is called the North Tor and the other, a little way off, the Summit Tor. A good place to rest, explore among the boulders and admire the excellent views.

Descend steeply from Slieve Bearnagh towards Slieve Meelmore, the Mourne Wall still on the R, taking a short path that veers away from the Wall to avoid the Bearnagh Crags. At the col

STARTING AND FINISHING POINT
At a car-park on the L of the minor road (312314). From Newcastle take the B180 (Hilltown road) forking L off it onto the unclassified but labelled Trassey Road 2.2 miles (3.5 km) west of Bryansford. Drive onward for 0.8 miles (1.3 km) to the car-park.

MAPS
Northern Ireland OS 1:50 000 Sheet 29, or 1:25 000 Sheet 'Mourne Country'.

LENGTH
7 miles (11 km)

ASCENT
2850 ft (870 m)

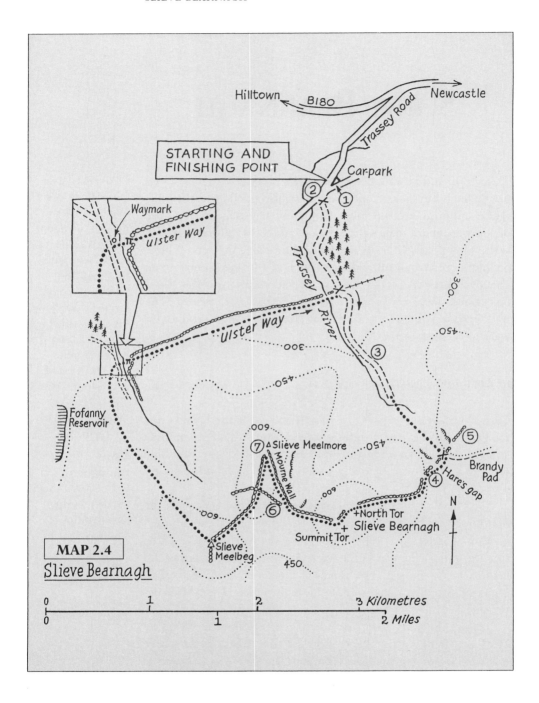

MAP 2.4
Slieve Bearnagh

continue along the Mourne Wall (not the other wall, which veers
L from it *(6)*) to reach the top of Slieve Meelmore
(2310 ft/704 m), crowned by one of the occasional towers along
the Wall *(7)*.

From Meelmore follow the Wall down to the col and thence

up to Slieve Meelbeg (2323 ft/708 m). Leave the Wall here to follow an intermittent and short-lived path down the north-west spur of Meelbeg with the Fofanny Reservoir prominent on the L and a wooded shore on the gentle slope behind it. Towards the bottom of the spur, veer R off it to meet an Ulster Way waymark, and follow the Way across a stream and over a stile.

Hare's Gap and the Mourne Walls

Continue on the Ulster Way, with a wall on the L, all the way to the second gate of the day. Surprisingly, in an area of generally clear paths, this section of the Ulster Way is intermittent and the ground underfoot wet. At the gate, turn L and follow the Way back to the metalled road. Turn R for the car-park.

1   The Cecil Newman Memorial
The simple stone memorial in the car-park commemorates Cecil Newman, a planner, who worked in the Northern Ireland Civil Service. He was among the first to recognize the necessity of planning for the mountain areas, particularly the Mournes.

2   *The Ulster Way*

This was the first Long Distance Route in the island, and is still by far the longest. The route is about 440 miles (700 km) long and goes right round Northern Ireland, taking in a wide variety of terrain. Most of it is waymarked.

3   *The 'Plug and Feathers' Method*

Look out along the way for wedge marks along the edges of granite stones. To split the quarried stones, rough holes were made in a line across the stone, and the plug (a small iron wedge) inserted between the feathers (two thin strips of steel).

4   *The Mourne Wall*

This sturdily built wall, the most noteworthy granite wall in a land of such walls, is 22 miles (35 km) long and encloses the catchment area of the Silent Valley Reservoir. It was built as late as 1910–22 by local unemployed men using locally quarried stones, which were transported by handbarrows, no animals being used. The route of the Wall was until recently that of the Mourne Wall Walk, which attracted annually such huge numbers that it has wisely been abandoned.

5   *Diamond Rocks*

A few hundred yards north-east of here are the Diamond Rocks where, if you have an abundance of patience, knowledge, skill and above all luck, you may chance upon almost worthless lodes of 'precious' crystalline stones such as topaz and quartz.

6   *The Stone Walls of Mourne*

Drystone walls, of which the Mourne Wall is the most notable example, are a common feature of the Mournes. Local farmers neatly constructed them of undressed granite stones and boulders. They served as a boundary for sheep pastures.

7   *Meelmore and Meelbeg*

'More' means big in Gaelic and 'beg' means small, but Meelmore is lower than Meelbeg by 13 ft (4 m). It is doubtful if the people who named the two mountains realized or would have cared about this seeming error. They probably named them on the basis of the apparent bulk as seen from where they lived.

The Tors on Slieve Bearnagh

3·5

GALTYMORE

STARTING AND
FINISHING POINT
At a turn-off on the
south side of the
southernmost of
the two Glen of
Aherlow roads
(872281). From
Cahir take the N24
(Limerick road)
branching L off it
after 6 miles (9.5
km) to follow signs
for Ballydavid
Wood Youth
Hostel. Do not turn
L to the Hostel;
instead continue
along the Glen of
Aherlow road. Pass
Condon's Pub on
the R and across a
bridge 1.7 miles
(2.7 km) beyond it.
Park on the waste
ground on the L.

MAPS
OS half-inch to the
mile series, and
both Sheets 18 and
22 are needed.

LENGTH
8 miles (13 km)

ASCENT
3400 ft (1040 m)

The northern slopes of the Galtees rise abruptly as a series of
broad spurs from the rich agricultural dairy lands of south Tipperary. South of these spurs the otherwise smooth form of the
high east–west grassy ridge that forms the backbone of the range
is disrupted by a line of surprisingly deep and dramatic corries.
By ascending one spur and descending another the walk includes
the highest peak of the range and its one Munro, taking in on the
way the rims of three of the best corries in the range.

ROUTE DESCRIPTION (Map 3.5)

Cross back over the bridge and take the second turn R, a narrow,
metalled road. Keep on this where forest roads leave to R and L.
On emerging from forest on the L (it continues on the R), and
with Cush ahead displaying great blocks of rock on its otherwise
smooth R flank, cross a fence L to walk uphill along a rough path
with fence and forest close on the L. Cross one fence near the
crest of the hill and turn R to follow the path towards Cush.
Continue upwards where the fence swings R and climb steeply
over grass, and near the summit between conglomerate boulders, to Cush (2109 ft/643 m).

Continue along the narrow ridge of Cush, and beyond it drop
to the boggy col towards Galtybeg (only at this point will the two
summits of Cush become evident). Climb over grass beyond the
col, fairly steeply at first and then more steeply, as far as Galtybeg, with the impressive corrie holding Borheen Lough on the
L. Galtybeg (2629 ft/801 m) commands excellent views, the
tiered cliffs of vertical rock in the next corrie, that of Lough
Diheen *(1)*, each topped by a precarious ramp of grass, being
particularly impressive. Drop to the col and from there climb to
Galtymore (3018 ft/920 m), signalled by a cairn, the lower part
of an OS obelisk and a white cross and memorial plaque *(2)*. The
view from here is exceptionally wide north and south, towards
the plains of Tipperary and beyond in one direction and towards
the Knockmealdowns in the other.

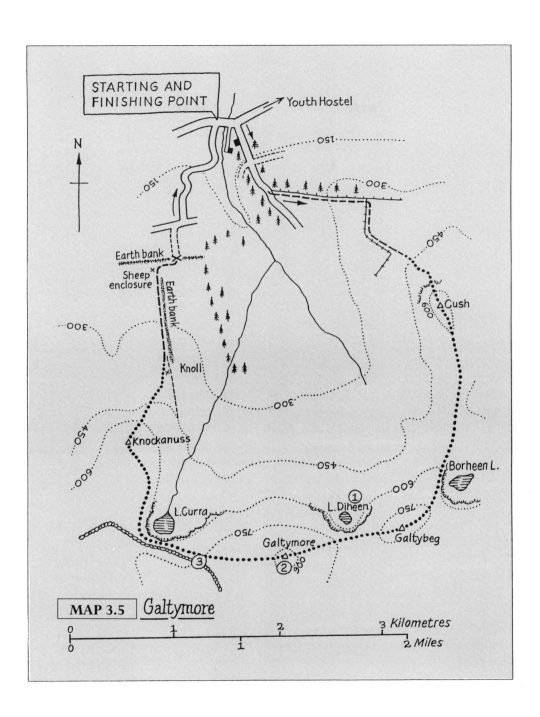

STARTING AND
FINISHING POINT

→ Youth Hostel

N

150

150

300

450

Earth bank

Sheep
enclosure

Earth bank

600

△ Cush

300

Knoll

300

450

△ Knockanuss

600

450

Borheen L.

600

① L. Diheen

750

L. Curra

750

Galtybeg

750

Galtymore

③

② 900

MAP 3.5 Galtymore

0 .... 1 .... 2 .... 3 Kilometres

0 .... 1 .... 2 Miles

The Galtees across the Glen of Aherlow

Continue to the western end of the summit ridge to a large cairn, dropping sharply beyond it to come within sight of a high wall *(3)*. Veer R to walk parallel to it, the corrie of Lough Curra on the R. Where the corrie rim veers R away from the wall follow the rim over the short climb to Knockanuss (2166 ft/660 m), descend along the spur north-west, veering R off it to pick up an earthbank near a small grassy knoll. Follow the earthbank down to enclosed land at a sheep enclosure. Turn R at another earthbank just beyond it and L through the first gate. Beyond it follow a track, which gradually improves to a metalled road as it gathers tributary lanes on its route down-hill. Follow the metalled road to the main road and the starting point.

1   *Lough Diheen*
    The corrie lake north-east of Galtymore attracted the rather gullible attention of the Halls, a husband and wife team who travelled around Ireland in the early 1840s. They uncritically re-told local stories that the lake was unfathomable, that if only a slight breeze blew across it the area round the lake became intensely cold, no matter how warm the day, and

that in spite of its apparent narrowness a stone could not be *Cush and Galtybeg*
thrown across it even when a champion in this simple sport
hurled it. All this the locals attributed to a Pooka (ghost)
which inhabited the lake. (A note for those interested in the
inconsequential: the lake is about 80 yards (70 m) across, a
considerable distance even for a champion stone-thrower.

2   *The Plaque on Galtymore*
The plaque on the summit commemorates James Blake and
Richard Hayward. James Blake was a local who, as the plaque
states, died while trying to rescue a woman bather in
Tangier. Richard Hayward was from far-off Belfast. He
wrote many books and guides between 1922 and his death in
1964, mostly, but not exclusively, about his native Ulster. It
is not clear why the men are jointly remembered in this way.

3   *The Stone Wall*
This wall was built late in the nineteenth century to keep
cattle away from the steep ground on the northern side of the
hills, and also perhaps to define grazing boundaries. It is quite
unusual for such a substantial wall to be built at this considerable height.

4·6

LUGNAQUILLIA AND THE GLEN OF IMAAL

STARTING AND
FINISHING POINT
In the Glen of Imaal
at a junction on a
side-road (982948).
Take the N81 to
the junction on the
east (L from
Dublin) for Donard
and go straight
through the village,
watching out for
the slightly offset
crossroads here.
Pass the Youth
Hostel and drive
straight ahead for
another 1.6 miles
(2.6 km) to a side
road R and
signboard on the L
reading 'WALKING
ROUTE FOLLOW'.
Park on the grass
around here.

MAPS
The OS 1:50 000
Sheet 56 map is
recommended. The
Wicklow District
one-inch to the
mile map is
adequate.

LENGTH
15½ miles (25 km)

ASCENT
3400 ft (1050 m)

Lugnaquillia at 3039 ft (925 m) is the highest mountain in Ireland outside Kerry, the qualification admittedly being extremely significant. It stands at the centre of a series of spurs reaching starfish-like in all directions and so allows a good variety of routes up one spur, down another. Though the summit is an unimpressive grassy plateau, the views it provides are excellent, particularly to the north. The high-level gradual descent in this direction, included in this route, extends and modifies these views and turns a simple mountain climb into an impressive circuit.

SAFETY NOTE
The area enclosed by this route is a military artillery range. Do not diverge to the L of the route. If firing is taking place, the whole area (including this route) will be out of bounds. Though firing is infrequent it is imperative that you check with the Army authorities before setting out: Tel: 0145–54626 or 0145–54653.

ROUTE DESCRIPTION (Map 4.6)

Facing away from the Army board, take the side-road south through an area of scattered trees past the memorial on the L *(1)*, over a bridge spanning the Little Slaney River and up to the hamlet of Seskin. Turn L here along a rough road which ends at a T-junction. Continue straight ahead through a gate onto a track marked by an occasional Army waymark. Walk steadily upwards on this track, which further on narrows to a path to reach the top of Camarahill (1567 ft/480 m), an undistinguished outlier of Lugnaquillia.
    Drop slightly beyond Camarahill, after which continue the steady climb, which steepens onto a rocky shoulder as the summit plateau of Lugnaquillia nears. Walk across the short grass to reach the huge cairn marking the summit at 3039 ft (925 m). The mountain indicator here points to an impressive array of

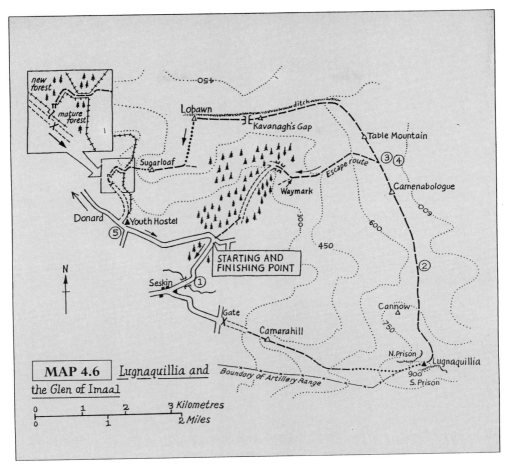

MAP 4.6 Lugnaquillia and the Glen of Imaal

peaks, including some in Wales. To obtain the widest panorama it is necessary to walk a little way from the cairn, an effort far outweighed by the consequent dramatic, broad views.

The descent from Lugnaquillia is an easy and scenic one. Walk north-east and then north-west, with the shoulder of Cannow to the L, so keeping to the high grassy ground. Along this initial stretch pick up a good path which continues all the way down to the boggy ground facing Camenabologue. On this gradual descent watch out for the rounded hills to the R of the path, whose high ground may mislead the unwary into wandering east. On a more cheerful note, look out also for the great whale-back peak of Tonelagee prominent ahead, and the tiny Art's Lough across a valley to the R of the route *(2)*.

From the low point climb Camenabologue (2495 ft/758 m) through a rocky area, and northwards beyond it descend through peat hags to the indistinct pass between the Glen of Imaal and Glenmalure *(3)*, *(4)*, a pass marked by Army signposts. Here you

35

may wish to return directly to the starting point. If so, take the clear path directly west following a line of Army waymarks down through open moorland, along an untidy forest road and through an area of pleasant deciduous trees to the start.

For the full route continue north at the pass to the cairn on Table Mountain (2302 ft/702 m), a mountain which lives up to its unflattering name all too well. Continue north-west from Table across a broad, windswept expanse of bogland, aiming for the long spur running west on the northern side of the Glen of Imaal. Along the initial stretch from Table, a wide but intermittent ditch develops, a useful aid in navigating all the way to Lobawn.

Once on the spur the route is generally downwards, the two rises being an unusually green unnamed hill east of Kavanagh's Gap and the rise to Lobawn itself (2097 ft/636 m), a grassy peak crowned by a WD (War Department) pillar. From Lobawn head on a dog-leg south and then west to Sugarloaf (1817 ft/552 m), following a clear path on the westward stretch. The descent from Sugarloaf is steep and gorse-impeded. Aim a little north of west and at forest turn L downhill to a point where the boundary fence is supplemented by horizontal wooden poles. Beyond these, two lines of fencing run directly into the forest (it is important to find this point). Cross the boundary fence and walk between the two lines of fencing on a narrow path, and beyond it keep close to the fence on the L. Turn L with this fence to a grassy track which can be reached using a stile.

Turn L onto the track and follow it on the level, and later downhill, first through deciduous and then through coniferous trees to a metalled road. Turn L here for a direct walk to the starting point (5).

1   *The Memorial in the Glen*
The memorial here honours four officers and 12 other ranks of the Irish Army who were killed at Leitrim Mountain near here in 1941. Twenty others were injured, 12 of them seriously. The accident occurred when a fuse failed during a demonstration of the operation of an anti-tank mine. Curiously, the report of this major accident in the local newspaper merited as much space as cake-making compet-itions in nearby villages. In 1979 three children were killed and nine injured in a shell explosion in this area while they were throwing 'scrap metal' around. Since then, security around the range has been greatly tightened.

The Glen of Imaal Artillery Range has been used by both the British Army in its time, and later by the Irish Army. On

Opposite: *Looking across the top of Glenmalure*

37

the walk you will see several 'WD' pillars, indicating the boundary of War Department territory.

2   *River Basin and Glacial Valley*
The contrast here between the broad, shallow river basin to the west (Imaal) and the deep, narrow glacial valley to the east (Glenmalure) is very striking. In this range as elsewhere glaciers tended to form on the north and east of the mountains, where shelter from the prevailing westerlies and the sun allowed snow to accumulate.

3   *The Pass between Glenmalure and Imaal*
Until the last century, coach and horse could use the track between the two glens and there was frequent communication between them. The track is now almost non-existent near the top of the pass to the east.

4   *Three Lakes*
The two lakes seen ahead are called 'Three Lakes'. If there ever was a third lake it has long since dried up.

5   *Irish Elk in Ballinclea Bog*
The skull and much of the antlers of an Irish elk (*Megacerous hibernicus*) were dug out of the bog near here during drainage operations in 1983. The elk, which lived 7000–10 000 years ago, was about the size of a horse, with antlers 12 ft (3.7 m) across.

Summit of Lugnaquilia

Introduction

This region comprises the large, sprawling county of Donegal and the area to its south in Sligo, which is geographically close but geologically far distant from it. Backing a rugged indented northern coast, the core of the region consists of the great ranges of hills, much of them over 2000 ft (610 m), stretching in parallel lines south-west to north-east; Errigal to Muckish, and the Derryveagh and Glendowan Mountains. Each range is bare and unforested and each separated from its neighbours by lowland bog or lake. The clear-cut orientation of these hills reminds one of the Scottish Highlands and no wonder, since they belong to the same mountain-building epoch. Indeed, not only the hills echo Scotland; the people of Donegal have more than a touch of the Scot about them in accent and in their forthright manner, accentuated by the seasonal migration to Scotland that has long been a tradition here.

South of this core area, in a wide band across the centre of Donegal, are lower and less rugged mountains degenerating in more than a few places into windswept moorland. In the south-west of Donegal is a great area of mountain bulging westward which includes the massive cliffs of Slieve League and, fronting Donegal Bay, a tangle of muted mountains and high ground which has just a trace still of the south-west to north-east trend of north Donegal. A route along the sea-cliffs at Slieve League has been omitted. Of course the cliffs are spectacular but it is essentially an unchanging spectacle with a dull landward side. In addition, access is difficult.

The scarplands and tiny but rugged hills of Sligo (and Leitrim) across Donegal Bay are quite different to any part of Donegal, or to anywhere else in Ireland for that matter. This is a gentle and less wild area with strong literary and poetic associations, though the attractions for the walker are far from minor.

Five walks in this area have been included. One representative sample from the Sligo area was essential, and the plateau of Ben Bulbin, the name widely associated in both poetic and mountaineering terms with the whole area, gives as good a walk as any and better than most.

The remaining few routes encompass the great heartland of north Donegal. The lake and Castle of Glenveagh, the focal point of a National Park, provides a rare opportunity for a short walk combined with a visit to an elegant house and gardens. The circuit of the Poisoned Glen is in the lofty Derryveagh Mountains and approaches the range from the north, so taking in the scarred cliffs almost surrounding the wild, strangely-named defile.

Errigal and Muckish are the two best-known mountains in Donegal. And deservedly so, because they are two fine peaks. Taken separately they do not form good, looped walks, but together they give a tough but highly attractive route. Lastly, on the rugged, indented coastline facing north against the Atlantic is a walk on Horn Head peninsula, one of several impressive promontories in the region.

GLENVEAGH

STARTING AND FINISHING POINT
At Glenveagh Castle (021209). The entrance to the National Park is on the R251/L82. A bus takes visitors from the entrance to the Castle. It does not operate in winter.

MAPS
The Park authorities issue an adequate one inch to the mile map. The better alternative is OS 1:50 000 Sheet 1.

LENGTH
6 miles (9.5 km) for the short route; 7 miles (10.5 km) for the long.

ASCENT
400 ft (120 m) for the short; 1100 ft (340 m) for the long.

ACCESS
Walking off paths may be restricted in winter. For details telephone 0174-37090.

Glenveagh Castle, the focal point of Glenveagh National Park, and the starting point of this walk, is an oasis of sophisticated civilization in a desert of natural wildness. The Castle and its gardens stand on the shores of Lough Veagh, which in turn occupies a long, straight, beautiful valley, almost entirely unwooded except for a plague of rhododendrons on the hillside. The whole atmosphere of the area is as much Scottish as Irish, a feeling enhanced by the red deer that roam the hillsides. Both the routes given explore the narrow main valley and even narrower side valley, in which mixed woodland softens the otherwise bleak valley floor. Both give views of the spectacular three-tiered Astelleen waterfall. The long route, in addition, samples the high moorland, so giving long views of neighbouring peaks for comparatively little effort.

ROUTE DESCRIPTION (Map 1.7)

Short route From behind the Castle *(1)* walk south-west on a clear track to the end of Lough Veagh; that is, keep it on the R *(2), (3)*. Just beyond it, past a small cottage tucked into the bank on the R, turn back L steeply uphill onto a side track not shown on the map issued by the Park authority. Keep on this to walk through a mixed wood and later into a narrow, open valley. Turn back where the track loses itself in rough wet country and retrace your steps to the Castle.

Long route Walk along the lake as described above, but continue straight ahead on the main track where the side track branches L. Pass to the R of the stalking cottage. Where the track swings L and then R and immediately passes a copse of beeches on the L, the first point where rhododendrons do not block the upper slopes, ascent L up a steep, wet, pathless hillside.

At the top, between the two muted peaks of Farscollop ('Scollops' on the Park authority's map), cross the narrow, flat saddle and descend on the other side into a very wet side valley of the main valley.

Turn L and walk along an initially treeless, pathless stretch which further on gives way to a mixed wood in a narrow steep-sided valley. Follow the track which gradually emerges, keeping to it as far as the main track. Turn R onto this for the Castle.

1   *Glenveagh National Park*
   The Park covers 24,600 acres (10,000 ha) and includes a long line of mountains running north-east from Slieve Snaght as well as lower ground to the south-east of Lough Veagh. Part of Errigal is a detached segment. The Interpretative Centre

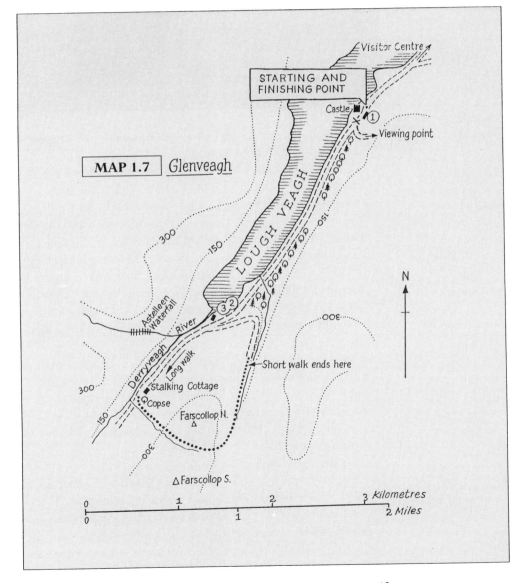

MAP 1.7 | Glenveagh

Lough Veagh

near the entrance car-park gives a fine overview of all aspects of the Park, including its geology and fauna and flora.

The Castle, a castellated four-storey mansion made from rough-hewn granite, was built about 1870 and it and its extensive gardens were donated to the state by its American owner in 1981. Both Castle and gardens are open to the public. It is a tribute to the attentive work of the planners and gardeners that a variety of exotic plants from as far away as Chile, Madeira and Tasmania thrive here in such unpromising and unlikely surroundings, sheltered by pines and rhododendrons. Sculptures and other formal features counterbalance the otherwise informal layout of the gardens.

2   *Derrybeg Bog*
The small bog at the south-west end of Lough Veagh is slightly dome-shaped like a raised bog, but its vegetation is more akin to that in a lowland blanket bog; that is, it is dominated by grass and sedge, and not shrub and moss as in the raised bogs. This bog has been classified as being of national importance.

3   *The Glenveagh Evictions*
Glenveagh was the scene of a notorious series of evictions in 1861. The landlord, John George Adair, evicted all 254 of his tenants in that year after a steward was murdered and sheep stolen. People horrified by these evictions paid the passage of the former tenants to Australia, where they founded a settlement named after their far-off native place.

Opposite: A stream in Glenveagh

44

2.8

HORN HEAD

STARTING AND
FINISHING POINT
At a side turn on
Horn Head
peninsula (017382).
Take the signposted
road off the N56 at
Dunfanaghy, drive
across Horn Head
bridge and park at
the side-road on L,
0.7 miles (1.1 km)
further on.

MAPS
OS 1:50 000 Sheet
2 is recommended.
Northern Ireland
OS Sheet 1 or
Republic of Ireland
OS Sheet 1 (both
half-inch to the
mile) are adequate.

LENGTH
7½ miles (12 km)

ASCENT
800 ft (240 m)

On a rugged coastline dominated by cliff-bound headlands and long, surf-fringed inlets, Horn Head peninsula is probably the most spectacular. Bounded on the east by Sheep Haven and the headland of Rosguill, and on the west by a long sweep of desolate shoreline reaching to Bloody Foreland, it offers excellent long views of sea-cliff and coastal scenery backed on the landward side by the high peaks of Muckish and its western neighbours.

The walk, one of several that can be easily devised on the peninsula, is along the more rugged eastern side. It starts quietly enough at sea-level. Gradually the tempo quickens along a low ragged coastline and over a shaggy headland until finally one faces the towering quartzite cliffs of Horn Head itself rising sheer 626 ft (191 m) from the surging ocean. The return is more placid; an easy stroll by road through the rough moorland at the centre of the peninsula.

SAFETY NOTE
The initial part of the route is difficult to follow in summer when the bracken is high. In addition, the pleasant walk along the beach at the start is severely restricted when the tide is in. If this is the case take the road, not the rough country behind the beach, to avoid an impassable stretch of vegetation.

ROUTE DESCRIPTION (Map 2.8)

Continue along the road that you arrive on *(1)* and descend to the beach where the road rises and continues straight ahead. Walk along the beach noting thick vegetation centred on a small stream which issues onto the beach *(2)*. Beyond it, climb the low, grassy slope and continue parallel to the shore, keeping it on the R.

A word about the long stretch from here to Horn Head. There are numerous paths wending here and there, each offering some help to the walker but none giving a definitive route. In the wild, rough and rising ground to the Head you must navigate without a sure path, a not over-difficult task given that the sea is always to

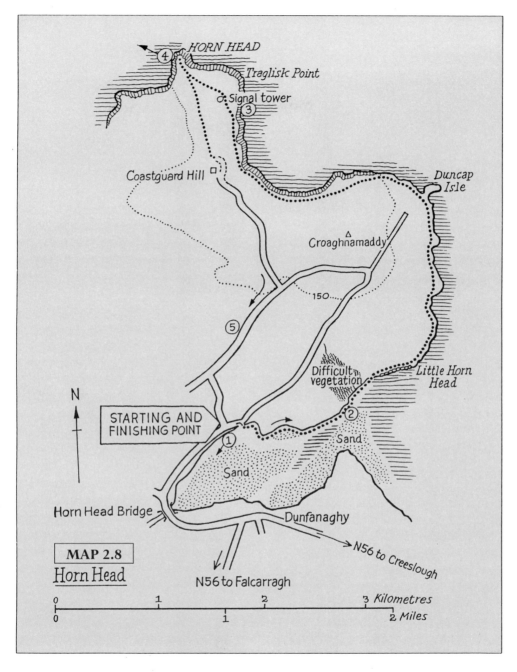

MAP 2.8

Horn Head

be kept on the R and that, in case of difficulty, there is generally a road not too far off on the L.

Follow a wall which runs parallel to the shore to an inlet on the R, and then continue past an amphitheatre sheltering an array of plants, which thrive in the comparatively calm ecosystem. Beyond this are a few curious, flat-topped islands and peninsulas. At the last of these, Duncap Isle, the coast swings from north to

west to reveal Traglisk Point with the ruined Signal Tower on its shoulder. After this turn, climb along the shoulder of Croaghna-maddy and beyond it continue along what is now a high cliff *(3)* past the Signal Tower. From here the two projecting peaks of Horn Head itself are a short distance away over short grass *(4)*.

To return, retrace your outward route keeping more to the R of the Signal Tower, over rough, boggy ground, and ascend towards (not to) the blockhouse on Coastguard Hill. Take the track which curls round the near side of the hill and walk the short stretch to a metalled road. Continue straight ahead where a road comes in on the L (this is the Horn Head scenic drive and is not shown on the maps) *(5)*. Turn L at the junction marked 'Horn Head 4 km' (the previous sign which measured the distance at 3 km is 1 mile/1.6 km away) and follow it downhill to the starting point.

1   *The New Lake*
    Horn Head peninsula was an island until as late as the eighteenth century, when the sand dunes to the south-west of the present peninsula developed. The area south of Horn Head bridge was a tidal estuary until the twentieth century, when it was sealed by westward-blowing sand encouraged by over-cutting of the marram sand at Tramore Strand. The OS maps still show the estuary, and not the freshwater New Lake which formed as a result.

2   *A Treacherous Coast*
    Note the wrecked ships half-buried in the sand around here.

3   *The Seabirds of Horn Head*
    The vertical or near-vertical quartzite cliffs here are a favourite nesting area for a variety of birds, including kittiwakes, guillemots, razorbills and puffins. Other birds which breed around here include the peregrine falcon, raven, rock pipit and chough.

4   *Tory Island*
    Tory Island, one of the most remote of the inhabited islands off the Irish coast, is visible from the Head on clear days, 9 miles (15 km) away to the west, its almost entirely cliff-bound southern side making it unmistakable. The islanders, who number about 200, are Gaelic-speaking.

5   *Fuchsia*
    The shrub fuchsia grows in unusual profusion along the hedgerows here, which are as thick and abundant as the fields they enclose are narrow and barren. Its red or purple bell-like flowers last from July all the way through to October.

Opposite: *Muckish from Horn Head*

49

BEN BULBIN

STARTING AND
FINISHING POINT
On a minor road
south of the Ben
Bulbin plateau
(714424). From
Sligo take the N15,
turn R at the
church in Rath-
cormack (signposted
'Glencar 4½'). Turn
R at the T-junction
after 1 mile (1.6
km) and park 1.4
miles (2.2 km)
further on near the
guesthouse.

FINISHING
POINT
On the same minor
road as above at a
crossroads at
689436. From the
starting point, drive
back for 1.9 miles
(3.0 km), to a
slightly offset
crossroads with a
metalled road R and
farm road L.

MAPS
OS 1:50 000
Sheet 16.

LENGTH
6½ miles (10.5 km)

ASCENT
1700 ft (520 m)

Ben Bulbin, an area immortalized by W. B. Yeats, is one of a group of plateaus to the east of Sligo town. From the lowlands the slopes below each plateau appear as a steeply rising grassy bank topped by a fearsome layer of dark limestone, so fearsome and forbidding that it is something of an anticlimax to discover that the plateau itself is flat moorland. It is as if the land that the maps optimistically labelled 'here be dragons' turn out to be solely the abode of slugs. However, the walk reaches the Ben Bulbin plateau by traversing one of the great gullies that cleave it open, on the way giving excellent views over scenic Glencar. Once there, one can admire a wide sweep of coast and the neighbouring section of the plateau's rim, though not the out-of-sight section at one's feet. The return is by a grassy slope and country roads.

SAFETY NOTE
The Ben Bulbin plateau is featureless, so it is difficult to fix one's position in bad visibility. It is also mostly surrounded by cliffs and steep ground. Fortunately, *most* of the cliffs are immediately evident because they are sheer and abrupt. Most also drop directly from the top of the plateau, so that the walker is unlikely to encounter cliffs low down on the descent, a disheartening experience. Nonetheless, care should be taken to avoid steep ground when coming off the plateau in poor visibility.

ROUTE DESCRIPTION (Map 2.9)

Go through the gate on the L of the guesthouse as one faces it and up the lane. Cross another gate further up and continue on to a derelict house. Here the lane ends so continue upwards across two rough fields, climb the steep but short rise beyond them and carefully cross the wall on the L into open country.

The good track into King's Gully is the next objective. With a plentitude of false trails hereabouts, perhaps the best plan is to head diagonally upwards *(1)* towards the gully, avoiding numerous rocks that have fallen from the cliffs above (especially if they are still moving). Once on the track, take it into the R side of the gully *(2)* and where it swings sharply back R continue straight ahead on a path, which peters out at about the same point as the gully softens to a steep but narrow valley.

Cross this valley onto the Ben Bulbin plateau *(3)*, a region of soft boggy ground and occasional peat hags, and head north-west (a compass bearing is advisable) to climb a rounded hill. Beyond it descend slightly to a narrow neck of high ground, keeping to the R of the promontory to admire the long stretch of coast round Donegal Bay.

Keep the cliffs on the R to Ben Bulbin (1722 ft/526 m). This has an OS obelisk which, if you didn't know that it was on a lofty site, would appear to be inexplicably located in a flat boggy field. From Ben Bulbin continue round the plateau, sheer cliffs still on

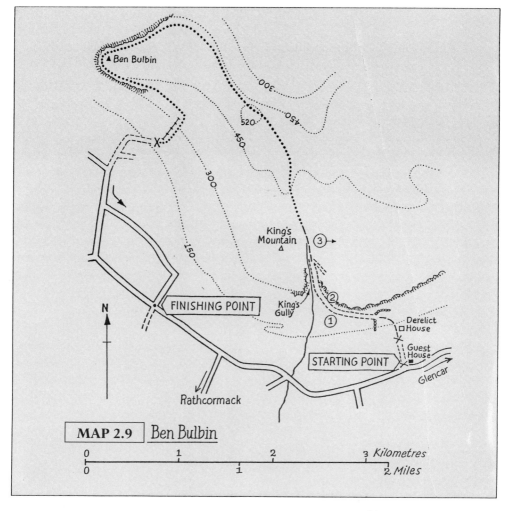

MAP 2.9 | Ben Bulbin

the R. Where they relent, drop gradually over rough ground to the upper end of a fence by an infant stream in a hint of a valley (in bad weather head to the R of the direct route, to make sure that you hit the fence). Follow the fence directly downhill on its far side to a grove of hawthorn and below it cross a gate on the R. Take the track beyond past a L turn (ignore it), and at a metalled road just ahead turn L (this may be better described as continuing straight ahead). Take the first side-turn L and follow it parallel to the rim of the plateau, and then directly away from it. The end of the walk is at the minor road (see STARTING POINT) which will now probably appear quite major.

1   *Drumcliff Church*
Sligo and the surrounding area was beloved of Ireland's national poet, W. B. Yeats, and it is in the little churchyard at Drumcliff 'under bare Ben Bulben's head' that he is buried (the spelling of 'Ben Bulbin' varies). The church tower is easily visible on this ascent at the north-east corner of Drumcliff Bay. Many of Yeats's most famous poems describe and indeed immortalize this area.

The prow of Ben Bulbin

2 *Flora on the Limestone Cliffs*

A wide variety of rare Alpine plants grows on the precipitous slopes of the limestone cliffs. For instance, this is the only site in the British Isles where the fringed sandwort grows. Other plants which thrive in this calcareous environment are mountain avens, alpine saxifrage and maidenhair fern.

3 *A Prehistoric Landscape*

A few miles to the east of here, on a continuation of the gently sloping plateau in County Leitrim, a huge prehistoric landscape of house sites, field systems and burial monuments has been discovered. This whole complex lies under blanket bog at 1300 ft (400 m), compared with present-day settlements which are seldom found higher than 500 ft (150 m). The complex is thought to have been inhabited by Neolithic people 5000 years ago.

Ben Bulbin and the King's Gully

2.10

THE POISONED GLEN

HORSESHOE

STARTING AND FINISHING POINT
At the hairpin bend on a side-road off the R251/L82 at Dunlewy (930192). From the Youth Hostel, drive east 0.9 miles (1.4 km), turning R here towards an unroofed church – it is a prominent landmark – from the R251, whether travelling east or west. Park at the hairpin bend near the church.

MAPS
OS 1:50 000 Sheet 1 is recommended. The Glenveagh National Park one-inch to the mile map is also satisfactory.

LENGTH
7½ miles (12 km)

ASCENT
2800 ft (850 m)

The Poisoned Glen, a morass of ominously green and watery vegetation, is almost surrounded by a line of bare rocky cliffs riven by deep dykes. The circuit of these cliffs is short in distance but not in time as the dykes extend as narrow but steep-sided rocky gaps in the plateau behind the cliffs, thus necessitating much exhilarating but time-consuming descending and climbing. The long views are excellent, dominated across Dunlewy Lough by the fine cone of Errigal which displays sometimes one, sometimes two of its tiny summits, and on a more practical level acts as a useful landmark for navigation.

ROUTE DESCRIPTION (Map 2.10)

From the church *(1)* take the track at the hairpin bend to a bridge 150 yards (135 m) away *(2)*. Cross it, turn L and follow the stream for about a ½ mile (1 km), at which point bogland on the R is a little less wet than further back. Leave the stream half R, striking directly towards Maumlack, carefully crossing the deer fence *(3)* marking entry to Glenveagh National Park on the way. Maumlack (1589 ft/484 m) is topped by an elegant, squared-off cairn. From the summit, walk east to keep to the high ground and then turn R (south) and drop to boggy terrain at Lough Beg. Climb over rough rocky ground to the unnamed peak directly to its south.

Here one enters a region of dykes, about which a general comment may be useful. The choice of route across this pathless region is infinite. However, the closer you are to the cliffs on the R, the harder the dykes are to negotiate — and the more spectacular the scenery. To the L, away from the cliffs, progress is faster but duller. The route described favours the R approach.

Cross the first dyke, climb the rocky promontory beyond it, and cross the second dyke along which the deer fence runs. Luckily the third dyke is also unmistakable because of the string of lenticular little lakes running along it. From this dyke climb steeply through crags, passing rock-bound Lough Maumbeg on

54

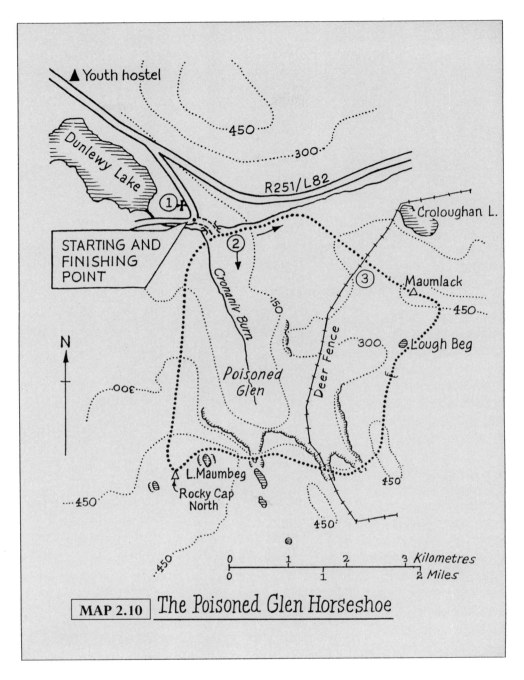

Dunlewy Lake

450

300

R251/L82

Croloughan L.

① ⊢

STARTING AND
FINISHING
POINT

②

③

Maumlack
△

450

N

Cronaniv Burn

150

Deer Fence

300

⊖ Lough Beg

Poisoned
Glen

300

450

△ L.Maumbeg

Rocky Cap
North

450

450

450

450

0   1   2   3 Kilometres
0   1   2 Miles

MAP 2.10 | The Poisoned Glen Horseshoe

the ascent to the northern summit of Rocky Cap, a peak to the
north-east of Slieve Snaght which is unnamed on the maps. This
peak has an undulating top so the summit cairn, and there is only
one, is useful. (NB If you encounter a second lake on this mountain you are on the way to the southern top and should retrace
your steps.)

From Rocky Cap descend north along a spur directly towards

Dunlewy (use the church as a target) down steep ground at first, then through a flat and boggy stretch with many tiny lakes, and finally over a surprisingly steep shoulder to the valley floor. Cross the Cronaniv Burn, walking upstream if necessary to ford it, turn L and walk back to the bridge and the hairpin bend.

1   *The Abandoned Church at Dunlewy*
     This Church of Ireland church was built in 1844, but was in full use for only a few years thereafter. After that, one service was held per *year* until 1955 when it was de-roofed and the door walled up. Even in the 1920s Arthur Fox, a scholar from Cambridge, noting that only three families worshipped there, added enigmatically that for that reason he 'would not be over-eager to worship in it'.

2   *The Poisoned Glen*
     From along this stretch of the route the glen is unmistakable on the R. The name is said to be derived from the poisonous Irish Splurge (genus Euphoria), which grew along the stream that drains the glen (very ineffectively). However, this explanation is somewhat implausible since it also grew in many other places. The valley is a glacial trough; a glacier originating in the Derryveagh Mountains to the south spilled over the cliffs surrounding the glen before heading first north and then along the lakes to the west of here.

     This area was one of the last in which the golden eagle bred; they were still being recorded as late as 1910. Alas, 20 years later eagles had departed from here and from Ireland generally. Some thought has been given recently to attempting to re-introduce them, but it is very likely that this would be unsuccessful as long as farmers continue to use pesticides.

3   *The Deer Fence*
     This fence is 28 miles (45 km) long, and thought to be the longest fence in the country. Erected in the 1890s it encloses most, but not all, of the National Park. The herd of 650 red deer which roam within the enclosed area is the largest in Ireland, but it has been introduced, and is not native as in Killarney.

The Poisoned Glen

ERRIGAL TO MUCKISH

STARTING POINT
On the R251/L82
east of Dunlewy at
940196. Drive 2.6
miles (4.2 km) east
from the Youth
Hostel and park at a
walking signpost on
the L. If driving
west, watch out for
the gate pillars
labelled 'Altan
Farm' on the R and
park at the signpost
a ½ mile (1 km)
further on.

FINISHING
POINTS
For the short route: At
the starting point
above.
For the medium route:
At Muckish Gap
(999269), at a
shrine on the
highest point of an
unclassified road
running south-east
from Falcarragh to
Glenveagh.
For the long route: At
the end of a side-
road off the N56
(008302). Take the
N56 west from
Creeslough for 1.8
miles (2.9 km), then
turn L onto the

Though they are otherwise sharply contrasted, Errigal and Muckish have this much in common: they are easily recognized. In fact, they are two of the most easily recognized mountains in Ireland.

They do not have much else in common. Errigal is a graceful quartzite cone with long scree slopes falling from a tiny double summit. Muckish is a long, gently sloping upland, a rock-strewn plateau standing high and conspicuous above the surrounding hills and low boglands.

Their locations, aloof from other high mountains, make it a little difficult to provide good looped walks encompassing each of them separately.

The solution is to combine them in a long south-west to north-east walk also taking in two of the Aghlas, a fine trio of peaks that lie between them.

This is the route of the Joey Glover Marathon (see page 61) except that the marathon goes north-east to south-west. The advantage of walking in the direction given here is that it allows an early 'out' for the faint-hearted, *after* the finest peak – Errigal – has been climbed (a second drop-out point at Muckish Gap is also indicated) and, no trivial consideration, it means that the strong prevailing westerlies are behind the walker.

It is hardly necessary to add that the coastal and mountain views on this route are superb and the underfoot terrain mostly (but not wholly) good. All that – and two options to drop out, should you be so foolish as to take either of them, make for an excellent walk.

SAFETY NOTE
The full walk is long with strenuous climbing, so an early start is essential. The cliffs and scree slopes at Mackoght and the Aghlas are not well represented on the maps, but are easy to avoid. The descent from Muckish requires your full attention at a time, late in a long day, when attention may be flagging.

ROUTE DESCRIPTION (Map 4.11)

Take the rough path across bogland towards Errigal following posts where the path is indistinct. At drier, steeper ground where the posts cease, follow the clear path upwards to a small cairn on a mound (useful later on in the route). Higher up climb, with steep scree on the R, to the Joey Glover memorial pillar *(1)*. Walk onward from here along a narrow path with ground falling steeply on both sides to the first summit of Errigal (2466 ft/751 m), which has the foundations of an OS obelisk. The second summit at about the same height is 30 yards (27 m) further on, reached by a narrow path. These are reputed to be the smallest summits in Ireland, a claim few would dispute. The views, especially towards the Derryveagh Mountains, are superb.

Retrace your steps as far as the small cairn mentioned above, and strike out from here to the L *(2)* to Mackoght (about 1600 ft/555 m) across rough, pathless country broken by occasional avoidable rocky outcrops. From Mackoght the next goal is the R-hand (i.e., eastern) end of Altan Lough. Bear R of the direct line to avoid cliffs and scree on the north-east side of Mackoght and also to avoid a shelving bogland, gentle on this side but craggy and steep where it overlooks the lough. The lough marks the first decision point.

Short route Take the clear grassy track on the near side of the stream entering the lough, walk to the R251/L82 at Altan Farm pillars, turn R and walk to the starting point.

Medium route If you wish to continue, cross the stepping-stones at the stream entering the lough, and with the curious castle-like derelict building on the L climb Aghla Mor keeping initially close to the lake to avoid a small drop further up on the direct route. Aghla Mor (1916 ft/584 m) – the alternative name 'Wee Errigal' might be more appropriately applied to Mackoght — has scree slopes to north-east and south-west and these come close together towards the summit to give a fine hogsback peak.

With these scree slopes in mind, retrace your steps a little and then descend steeply to the peat hags on the south side of Lough Feeane, and walk along the broad saddle south of the lake. Climb through the boulder field to the more southern (of two) Aghla Begs (about 1900 ft/603 m). From here swing slightly R of the direct approach again, to reach the south side of Lough Aluirg where there is but a narrow passable strip between the lake on the L and the forestry plantation on the R.

side-road (if coming from the other direction turn R just beyond the cemetery on the L of the road). Drive straight ahead for 3.6 miles (5.8 km) and park where the metalled road ends.

MAPS
OS 1:50 000 Sheet 1 for the short route and both it and Sheet 2 for the other routes are recommended. The OS half-inch to the mile Sheet 1 is satisfactory.

LENGTH
6½ miles (9.5 km) for the short route; 9 miles (14.5 km) for the medium route; 12 miles (19 km) for the long route

ASCENT
2800 ft (850 m) for the short route; 4800 ft (1460 m) for the medium route; 6100 ft (1860 m) for the long route

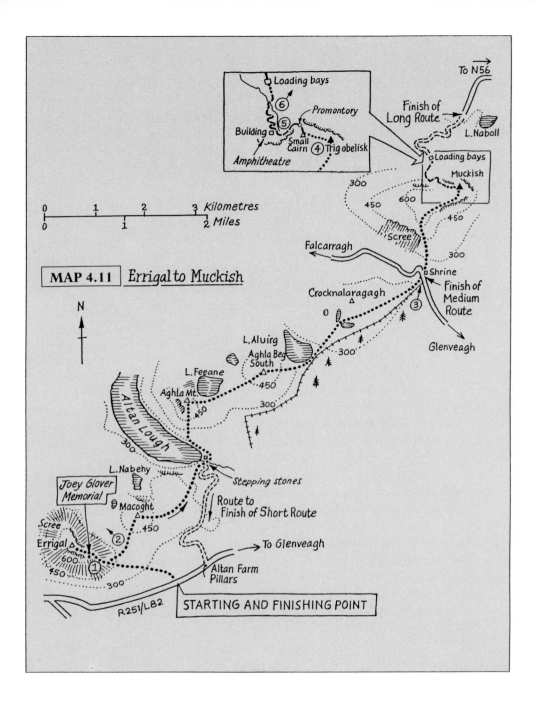

The next section poses a navigational problem. The hummocky, wet high ground to the north-east contains an indistinct peak, Crocknalaragagh, and three lakes, which are better navigational landmarks than the mountain. Across the entire area runs a meandering fence which, if it remains as it is at present, leads to the central lake. But will it? Perhaps it will collapse, be moved or be augmented by other fences, so leading to errors. The best plan is probably to rely on one's own resources. Aim for the small area between the two eastern lakes by climbing steeply at first and then walking over flat boggy ground. Ignoring Crocknalara-gagh, walk between the two lakes and climb a little to gain a distinct ridge (it has forest further down, close on its R) that runs all the way down to Muckish Gap *(3)*. This is the second drop-out point and marks the end of the medium route.

Long route If you intend to complete the long walk cross the road, go round to the L of the mound which shelters the shrine to take the rough path which ascends a spur terminating about 1000 ft (300 m) above on Muckish plateau. Walk across the gently sloping plateau, keeping to its south-east edge to avoid rocky ground, to reach the OS obelisk marking the summit *(4)*.

The next task, an essential one, is to find the way down, which both here and at the quarry below requires you to keep to paths that give a safe way down the rough steep ground. From the obelisk head west for about 220 yards (200 m) to a small cairn and follow a faint path half R which originates about here and bends L over a promontory bounded by cliffs and steep ground to R and L.

This path ends at the quarry, which takes the form of a small semi-amphitheatre in a spot likely to excite considerable awe *(5)*. It consists of a tiny sandy plain, rusting mining artifacts and curious light-brown towers fronting the partly man-made cliffs which half surround the quarry. The only sound, as likely as not, is the harsh caw of the ravens fluttering overhead.

Let not awe cause a hasty descent. Walk to the ruined building at the centre of the rim of the quarry and take the miners' path which is to its R (facing out) and to the L of a small stream. The path follows stumps of iron fence posts and decayed wood poles which occasionally peter out. In case of doubt, remember that the path runs wholly *between* two streams and crosses a sand run at *one* point only *(6)*.

At a tiny valley on level ground, clogged with discarded rocks, cross the stream on the R and descend steeply and directly to the loading bays visible below. Take the grassy quarry road which begins at the bays, climbing the boulders across it a little way down to follow the clear rocky quarry road below them to a metalled road, where the route finishes.

1   *The Joey Glover Memorial*
    The simple cairn and plaque here are in memory of Joey Glover, a great mountaineering enthusiast, whose special love was for these, his local mountains. He was murdered in

1976 by the Provisional IRA in one of their many 'mistakes'.

2   *Drumlin Country*
The curious cluster of tiny oval hills seen to the L on the low ground between Errigal and Mackoght appears to be drumlins formed by the passage of moving ice. Most are grassed, but this cluster is of rough stone.

3   *Muckish Gap*
This is a glacial breach, the most spectacular of several along the line of mountains from Errigal to Muckish. The col was once 400 ft (120 m) higher, but ice moving north from the Derryveagh mountains broke through the low point here to form this impressive gap.

4   *The Disappointments of Caesar Otway*
Caesar Otway, the splendidly named intrepid Victorian traveller, climbed Muckish in the 1820s. After four hours (sic!) exertion he neared the top. 'I ran, covered with perspiration and panting with heat, to mount the topmost ridge; and just as we arrived there . . . and began to feast on the immense vision of the earth and ocean beneath us, a vast murky cloud from the Atlantic, big with sleet and moisture, enveloped us as well as the whole top of the mountain as with a night-cap, and made every thing so dark, indistinct, and dreary, that we could scarcely see one another.'
Some things never change.

5   *The Mine Workings of Muckish*
Fine-quality white quartzite sand (99.5 per cent silica) used in the manufacture of spectacles, was mined here until 1955, when the workings became uneconomic. The path to the upper workings used by the miners was obviously well made, but is now ruined.

6   *The Letterkenny and Burtonport Extension railway*
The grassy embankments marking the route of this disused line can be clearly seen on the descent. The L&BER was a narrow-gauge railway running from Letterkenny in a meandering curve to the town of Burtonport on the west coast of Donegal, and was primarily intended as a means of developing the fishing industry there. The route was a difficult one — mostly unyielding granite rock — or, equally difficult, too-easily yielding soft bogland. Opened in 1903, the line closed in 1940.

The route from Errigal

INTRODUCTION

The mountains of the West, that is, of the counties of Galway (pre-eminently), Mayo and Clare, are located in small, distinct groups separated by low passes and long valleys. Access is good, given the scattered nature of habitation which clings to the narrow fringe between ocean, bogland and mountain. From Clifden, the core area to the east is but a short drive away so the roads, though generally poor, do not have to be endured for very great distances.

The most obvious characteristic that all these discrete mountain ranges have in common is that, to use an Irishism, they are all different! Bleak, flat, boggy upland, limestone terraces, fine rocky conical peaks, upland plateaux with cliffy flanks, grassy hills ending in sea-cliffs, are all represented here. This meant that the selection of routes was quite simple. What was required was just one route in each of the best ranges coupled with a firm resolve not to include that almost as good or nearly as satisfying *second* route in each range. The routes therefore almost chose themselves.

The one range where it was most tempting to choose a second route was the Twelve Bens. What a bewitching magical group — a tiny but crowded canvas of conical peaks in bare rocky splendour, soaring skyward so that it is almost impossible to accept that the highest peak is less than 2400 ft (730 m) high. The route chosen is the most spectacular classic.

The Maamturks lie just across the Inagh valley from the Bens. To quote a well-used and observant phrase: they are the Bens straightened out and with the tops sheared off. It is indeed true that the tops barely rise above a rocky quartzite plateau and that the range more or less orients itself in a narrow line. This latter characteristic makes good circuits almost impossible to devise. With this limitation in mind, a route has been chosen to one of the cols that cause such anguish to those hardy souls doing a full traverse of the range, with a return along the Western Way.

There is a route for potterers, in a very distinct area just south of the fiord of Killary Harbour, the great divide between Connemara (western Galway) and the mountains of Mayo,

which is navigationally easy and scenically a delightful *Doo Lough and*
juxtaposition of coast and hillside. *Mweelrea*

North across Killary Harbour is Mweelrea, at a modest
2688 ft (814 m) the highest mountain in the entire area. The
Mweelrea massif, for Mweelrea is one of a group of hills rising
from a plateau, is the best of three ranges, sectors of a great circle
of mountains split by north-south and centre to east passes. Of
the several routes considered onto the summit plateau (including
one by boat across Killary!) this one traverses the rim of the
corrie cleaving the eastern side of the massif. A memorable
excursion that, like some of the others, almost chose itself.

Finally, on the outskirts of the West two greatly contrasting
walks: Achill Island provides a comparatively easily accessible
cliff walk in an area which has many that are far from accessible
— and it also happens to be one of the most memorable; the
Burren is unique in Ireland — a strange area of limestone slabs
which shelters a bewildering range of rare and varied flora.

Mention should perhaps be made of Croagh Patrick, a notable
omission. Croagh Patrick is Ireland's 'holy' mountain, an attri-
bute which has blighted it with an ugly scar of a pilgrimage track
and squat chapel on the summit. It is probably better to leave it
to the penitential multitudes, and seek spiritual solace on
unspoilt and less-frequented hills.

65

1·12

KILLARY HARBOUR

STARTING AND
FINISHING POINT
At Killary Harbour
Youth Hostel
(769651) in Rosroe
on the southern
shore of the fiord.
From Leenane take
the N59 towards
Clifden turning R
after 4.4 miles (7.0
km) (this is the
second side-turn
within a few
hundred yards on a
road which has no
side-roads on this
side after Leenane).
Continue along the
length of Lough Fee
and 0.2 miles (350
m) beyond it fork R
uphill. The Hostel
is 1.8 miles (3.0
km) further on.

MAPS
Both the 1:50 000
Connemara map
and OS 1:50 000
Sheet 37 are
recommended.

LENGTH
5 miles (8 km)

ASCENT
400 ft (120 m)

This is an easy walk nearly all of which is on a clear path or track
with little climbing. The route is along the shore of a narrow
fiord, by far Ireland's best (though some would say that it is
Ireland's *only* true fiord). Across the waters the great southern
wall of Mweelrea rises unbroken from shore to summit, 2600 ft
(800 m) of grassy slopes. A good walk for a day of low cloud, but
nonetheless it would be a pity to miss the full glory of the excellent sea and mountain scenery.

ROUTE DESCRIPTION (Map 1.12)

Walk along the road away from the Hostel *(1)* and the tiny harbour beside it, turning L onto a track just before the first house
on the L. Follow this upwards ignoring the gate on the L set in a
stone wall which runs beside the track for a short distance. A
little further on, Killary Harbour *(2)* is fully revealed. Look out
on the opposite shore for the remains of a pre-famine village *(3)*.

Route-finding from here is simple, with one proviso vital for
the return. Watch out for the deserted house (rough definition: a
deserted house is roofed, a ruin is not) half-hidden in rhododen-
dron, and note also the lateral gated wall beyond it. Between
house and wall search carefully for a green track heading back.
Though barely more than a gently sloping stretch of grass amidst
steeply rising ground, it is a stretch of grass that runs surrepti-
tiously slightly uphill and almost parallel to the good track that
you are on. Note this for the return carefully.

For now, continue along the coast, cross a concrete bridge
over a stream which descends briskly as a series of low waterfalls
(a good place for a picnic) and pass the ruin on the L, the first on
the fiord side. Around here the south-east outlier of Mweelrea
descends in a diminuendo of rocky hillocks into Killary and the
end of the Maamturks increasingly dominates the skyline beyond
it. On the near side, old oaks shelter in a slight hollow ahead.

There is nothing to stop further onward wandering, but the
best of the scenery is behind. For the return take the track L

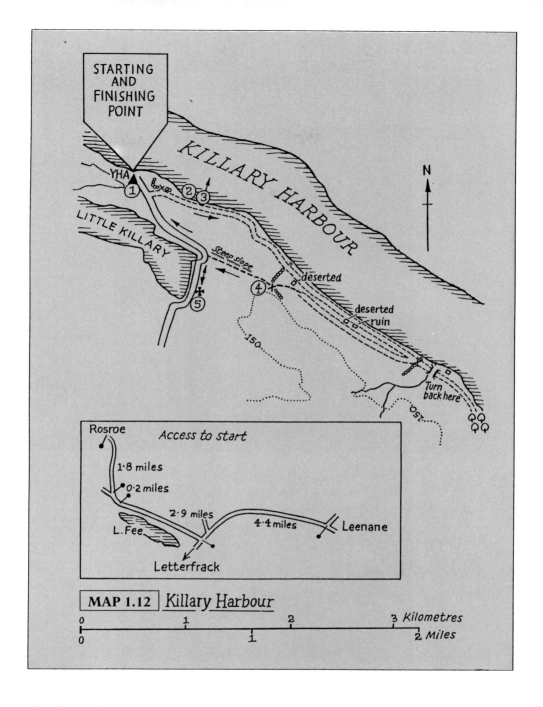

STARTING
AND
FINISHING
POINT

KILLARY HARBOUR

YHA

LITTLE KILLARY

Steep slope

deserted

deserted
ruin

150

Turn
back here

Rosroe   Access to start

1·8 miles

0·2 miles

2·9 miles

L. Fee   4·4 miles   Leenane

Letterfrack

| MAP 1.12 | Killary Harbour |

0 .... 1 .... 2 .... 3 Kilometres

0 .... 1 .... 2 Miles

already noted, and follow it to near a deserted house set at right
angles to the shore. Just before this house the track inexplicably,
but fortunately only temporarily expires at a wall that must be
crossed. Beyond the house it resumes resolutely uphill, no longer
meekly paralleling its coastal companion. The path ends at a
corner in a stone wall. Take a gate on the L here and follow the
fence beyond steeply uphill along a curious rocky escarpment *(4)*

67

Killary Harbour Youth Hostel

running close by on the R. At the crest the delightful Little Killary Harbour comes into view. From here continue steeply downhill to the road.

At the road turn L to visit the tiny Church of Ireland church *(5)* tucked in behind a high wall on the L a few hundred yards away. Afterwards retrace your steps to the starting point.

1   *A Philosopher at Killary*
    The Youth Hostel was the temporary home of the philosopher Ludwig Wittgenstein after World War II (of course it was not a hostel then). Here he wrote his book *Philosophical Investigations*.

2   *Killary Fiord*
    During the Ice Age, a glacier pushed its way out to sea hereabouts along an existing river valley, deepening it from a shallow V to the deep U of the present-day fiord and leaving a bar at the entrance, the equivalent of a moraine. The fiord is deeper at the landward end.

The shoreline at Killary

The shelter provided by the hills and the unusually deep water in the harbour have made it a centre for mussel farming. The mussels cling to long ropes hanging from the rafts. Apart from being unsightly, questions have recently been asked about the chemical effects of this type of intensive fish-farming.

3   *A Pre-famine Village*
The pre-famine village across the fiord and clearly visible from this side was called Uggool. Tillage beds climb the steep and infertile hill behind the village, indicating how desperate the plight of the land-starved peasants was in the 1830s and 1840s.

4   *The Escarpment*
The curious cliff and trench here was caused by the rubbing of a chain which the devil was pulling to drag away Saint Roc, a local holy man. If that is too difficult to believe, the alternative explanation is that it is a thrust fault caused by the movement of one body of rock relative to a contiguous body. (How dull science is compared to popular theology!)

5   *The Church at Salrock*
The small Church of Ireland church maintained a curious custom in the past. Mourners at funerals smoked clay pipes after the religious service and these were heaped in the graveyard. Two plaques on the inside wall remember two brothers, both born during World War I and killed in World War II. It must have been a heavy sacrifice not only for their parents, but for the tiny Protestant community of the area.

Killary Harbour and Mweelrea

ACHILL HEAD

STARTING AND
FINISHING POINT
Keem Bay (560045)
at the western end
of Achill Island.
Take the N59 to
Mulrany and there
take the R319/L141
to Dooagh. Con-
tinue onwards to
the road head at
Keem Bay where
there are several
large car-parks.
Leave plenty of
time for the drive
as the roads are
generally poor.

MAPS
OS 1:50 000 Sheet
30 is recommended.
OS half-inch to the
mile Sheet 6 is
satisfactory.

LENGTH
5 miles (8 km)

ASCENT
1100 ft (340 m)

Achill (pronounced '*Ack-ill*') is the largest island off the coast, though its insular status is impaired as it is joined to the mainland by a road-bridge. The island is shaped like a right-angled triangle, its most acute angle at Achill Head jutting out defiantly west into the Atlantic. Sea-cliffs dominate the two sides near this angle, low to the west of Keem Bay where the walk starts but rising to nearly 2200 ft (690 m) under the summit of Croaghaun Mountain further north. Between Keem and Achill Head the walk takes in some of the most breath-taking sea-cliff scenery in Ireland. Although the route does not include Croaghaun, the sweep of cliffs under that mountain can be seen clearly from Achill Head — ironically they cannot be seen from Croaghaun itself.

ROUTE DESCRIPTION (Map 1.13)

Before starting it might be of interest to consider the surroundings. Keem Bay is tucked into a bowl of mountains unbroken except for the ocean and the coastal strip whence you drove *(1)*. The curious aspect is that nearly the entire sweep of hills around is 'one-sided': the sides hidden from here terminate abruptly either in sea-cliffs or corrie wall. Thus the surroundings uncannily mirror St Kilda, far west of Scotland in the Atlantic.

From the bay *(2)* climb over pathless grass to the top of Moyteoge Head to the south-west, which is crowned by the look-out post clearly visible from the bay. Once there navigation is easy. Turn R and walk north-west towards and over the two great waves of rising ground ahead which fall on the L to the sea in dramatic sea-cliffs. As you advance, the bulky but dull shoulder of Croaghaun (2192 ft/688 m) increasingly dominates the view. A little further on, the high but not sheer cliffs falling from its summit to the sea with the curve of the Belmullet peninsula behind, can be clearly seen. In spite of their height these cliffs are not as impressive as the Achill Head sea-cliffs to the L and further on also to the R.

The cliffs on Achill Head converge gradually to a knife-edge

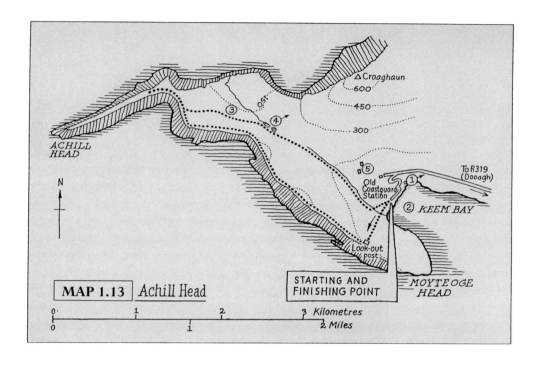

MAP 1.13 Achill Head

STARTING AND
FINISHING POINT

0   1   2   3 Kilometres
0   1   2 Miles

and conditions on the day (for example, wind and the slipperiness of the rocks) combined with the walker's burgeoning fear of an unscheduled visit to the slowly pounding sea far below will eventually dictate a retreat. When prudence advises, turn back and initially retrace your steps, with the cliffs now on the R. Where feasible, descend gradually L from the cliffs, walk upstream roughly parallel to a westward-flowing stream *(3)* below on the L and, when they come into view, head to two small lakes at the col between the Achill Head cliffs R and the rising featureless flank of Croaghaun L *(4)*.

From these lakes continue in roughly the same direction (south-east) to pick up a stream, noting at the start of this stretch the distinctive cone of Croagh Patrick ahead neatly framed by Croaghaun and Moyteoge Head. Follow this stream downhill back to the car-park at Keem, passing on the way two imposing ruins *(5)* and an equally imposing deserted house, the latter the old coastguard station.

1   Amethysts at Keem Bay
    On the last ridge on the road into Keem, amethysts were discovered in the 1960s in the course of constructing the present road to the bay. The clear purple gemstone can still be found with a little patient searching.

Achill coastline with Achill Head in the distance

2 *Shark fishing at Keem Bay*

Keem Bay was a centre for the shark-fishing industry for 25 years up to the mid-1970s. Basking sharks up to 35 ft (10 m) long and weighing up to 6 tons (tonnes) were caught in nets attached to the cliffs and were then killed by harpoon from curraghs, the fragile row-boats traditional on the Atlantic coast. It must have been a gory business. Only the sharks' liver oil and fins were used, the latter being exported to the Far East.

3   *Booleys*   *Keem Bay*

The oval, stone-wall enclosures along this stream are good examples of *booleys*, shelters which cattle-minders inhabited in the summers while their bovine charges grazed on the summer pastures. Achill is the last place in Ireland where this practice survived.

4   *The Views of Eric Newby*

Eric Newby, the noted English travel-writer, climbed Croaghaun in his youth. Many years later, as described in his book, *Round Ireland in Slow Gear*, he climbed it again. He had exactly the same view on the two occasions — zero visibility caused by low cloud — so it is unlikely that even the not-easily-discouraged Newby will ever come to believe in third time lucky.

5   *Captain Boycott*

These ruins, a substantial house and store, were built around 1857 by Captain Boycott, a local landlord. He later moved east to the Mayo mainland where he achieved unwanted fame by becoming the original victim of the effective protest action named after him.

THE BURREN

STARTING AND
FINISHING POINT
At or near the side-
turn off the R477/
L54 at Fanore
(144088).

MAPS
T.D. Robinson's
stylish and artistic
map *The Burren*, on
a scale of 1:35 200
(1.8 in to the mile),
while otherwise
unsurpassed, is
uncontoured. The
alternative is the
OS half-inch to the
mile Sheet 14.

LENGTH
9½ miles (15 km)

ASCENT
1500 ft (460 m)

The Burren of north-west Clare, 60 square miles (160 square km) of karstic country, is quite unlike any other in Ireland. From a distance the hills, which rarely rise over 1000 ft (300 m), look like a pile of stacked grey plates, each smaller than the one below it. Close up, the landscape is almost lunar, a set of platforms composed of flat slabs of limestone broken by long, narrow grooves called grikes. Each platform ends in a short cliff above which is another grey platform.

The botanic and archaeological variety of the Burren matches its scenic weirdness. Plants of widely diverse origins thrive in the lime-rich patches of soil, or shelter in the narrow crevices of the grikes. Sites from many eras from Stone Age to medieval dot the hills.

In such an area the walker might prefer to wander freely rather than be constricted by a formal walk. The walk given here has at least the virtue of providing most of the elements which make the Burren what it is: the limestone terraces and cliffs, the varied flora and archaeology, the excellent coastal views of Galway Bay and beyond, as well as commonplace fields and quiet country roads.

ROUTE DESCRIPTION (Map 2.14)

Walk north, that is, with the coast on the L, along the coast road, the R477/L54 and turn first R up a track. Where the track swings sharply R at a bungalow on the R, turn L off it along a wisp of a path. Continue roughly on the level as it improves to a wide track between stone walls that rises gradually across the hillside. Cross three stone walls (carefully) on this almost imperceptible ascent and after the third, where the track divides, take the R branch. Turn R off it after a short distance (*1*) where it levels off, so heading directly and pathlessly for the great ringfort of Caher-doonfergus (*2*) across the limestone pavements.

From the ringfort head directly to Dobhach Bhrainin (1045 ft/319 m), climbing several terraces on the way (this is a

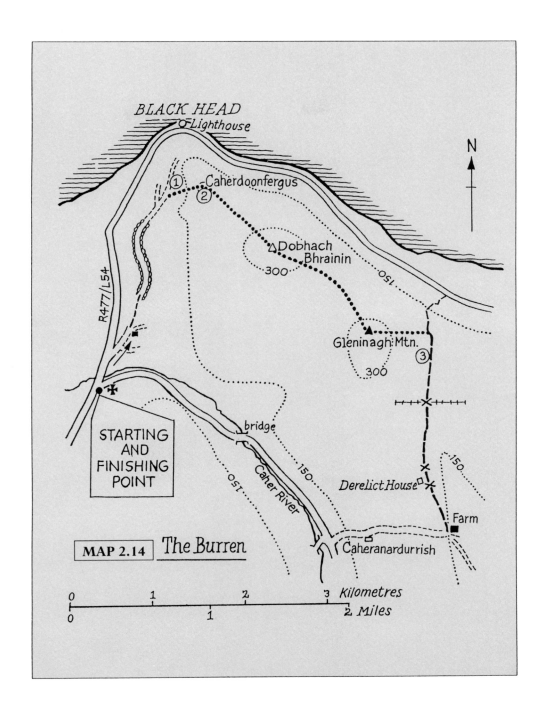

BLACK HEAD

Lighthouse

R477/L54

① Caherdoonfergus

②

△Dobhach
Bhrainin

300

150

▲ Gleninagh Mtn.

③

300

STARTING
AND
FINISHING
POINT

bridge

Caher River

150

150

OSI

OSI

Derelict House

Farm

MAP 2.14 | The Burren

Caheranardurrish

| 0 | 1 | 2 | 3 | Kilometres |

| 0 | 1 | 2 | Miles |

N

constant feature until after Gleninagh). The top is marked by a
small cairn, a useful edifice in flat terrain. Descend to the pass
towards Gleninagh Mountain so avoiding grassy hollows on the
direct route, and ascend directly to Gleninagh, which is the same
height as Dobhach Bhrainin, and is marked by an OS obelisk.

Descend to the pass to the east and at it turn R along a track that is difficult to find at the pass itself but is clear a little way down. This track deteriorates to a path through fields in the high grassy Gleninagh South valley *(3)*, scrub and limestone slabs on both sides. Cross a wall and at the gate just beyond, where you may by now have concluded that the path is purely imaginary, head towards a derelict house visible to the R of the valley, picking up the path again closer to it. Take the good track which originates at the house to what appears to be a crossroad (though the L branch terminates at a nearby farm) and turn R uphill here along another track, passing Caheranardurrish, reputedly a sheeben and church, just over the crest.

Descend on a winding course, still on the track, to a metalled road. Turn R onto it and walk steadily downhill all the way to the coast road.

1   *Flora of the Limestone Slabs*
    Bloody cranesbill, mountain avens and spring gentians are among the many plants from the Arctic, Alps and Mediterranean which grow here on the calcium-rich soil. Maidenhair and hart's tongue fern thrive in the micro-environment of the sheltering grikes. These plants and many others are best seen in the late spring when the flowers are blooming.

2   *Caherdoonfergus*
    Caherdoonfergus, or as T. D. Robinson's map sternly puts it, 'Cathair Dhuin Irghuis, miscalled Caherdoonfergus', is a fine example of a large ringfort. This formerly lightly wooded area of well-drained land once attracted a large population, as the many ringforts in the Burren testify. Overgrazing and possibly a climatic change led to erosion and the subsequent uncovering of the bare rock.

3   *The Valley of Gleninagh South*
    This area is a fertile contrast to the bare hillside on both sides. The soil is composed of thick glacial deposits which accumulated in the valley. At the end of the walk along the Caher River a cross-section of similar deposits has been exposed by subsidence into the river.

Limestone pavements

THE CENTRAL MAAMTURKS

STARTING AND
FINISHING POINT
The car-park on the
north-east side of
the R344 (Lough
Inagh road) 5 miles
(8 km) from
Kylemore and 5½
miles (9 km) from
Recess (847533).
The car-park is
signposted
'Mamean Tobar &
Leaba Phadraig' in
archaic Irish
lettering. If your
knowledge of this
lettering is rusty,
look for the sign for
Lough Inagh
Fishery directly
opposite.

MAPS
Both the 1:50 000
Connemara map
and OS 1:50 000
Sheet 37 are
recommended.

LENGTH
9 miles (14.5 km)

ASCENT
2750 ft (840 m)

Like other sections of the Maamturks, the rock-ribbed central section, which is the focus of this walk, runs from one high pass to another in a long, gently curving line. Ascending the rock-strewn plateau above, it takes in two major peaks which, depending on the exact point from which they are viewed, rise above the plateau with varying degrees of success. The panorama from the tops, particularly towards the crowded peaks of the Bens, is excellent. The walk reaches the lowlands along a tiny river valley and ends as it began along the Western Way.

ROUTE DESCRIPTION (Map 3.15)

From the car-park leave the R344 to follow the minor road uphill, thus emulating the route of the pilgrims to Mamean (1). Continue along the part-metalled part-pot-holed road (2) passing through the scattered houses at Illion West/An Uillinn Thair after 1½ miles (2.5 km), and at the dip beyond it where stone walls clamber in a higgledy-piggledy way among rising ground on the L look out beyond them and before the river for a place where there is comparatively dry ground on which to start the walk to Mam Ochoige, a high pass in the Maamturks.

Walk upriver towards the pass keeping to the L bank, and pass through the huge, dark rocky ramparts guarding the pass by taking the only significant gap, that taken by the stream. Beyond is level ground, an ideal spot for rough camping. From here, continue steeply uphill to the pass (3), where the lake shown on the maps is nowhere to be seen. You have not located the wrong gap however. The mystery will soon be revealed.

The route from the pass to the first peak, Knocknahillion/Cnoc na hUilleann (1993 ft/607 m) is a straightforward climb through rough vegetation and scattered boulders. Look back on this ascent to see the sought-for-lake lying just above the gap. This climb also affords good views down into the long, grassy-sided Failmore Valley to the R and behind.

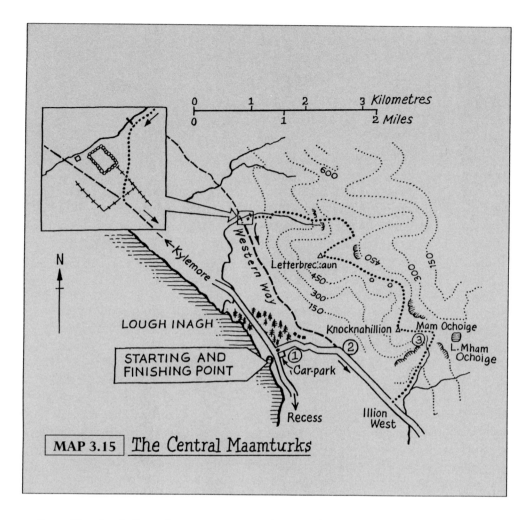

MAP 3.15 | The Central Maamturks

From Knocknahillion the route runs north over a bewildering rocky landscape of tiny hillocks and hidden lochans, narrowing at one point to a narrow but flat neck. Beyond this a bulky cairn beckons — the top of Letterbreckaun/Binn Briocain? Alas, no. It marks the edge of the virtual plateau on which Letterbreckaun (2193 ft/669 m) lies. Having gained this plateau note another cairn, and then another. Exactly which one marks the top is difficult to say with certainty. While this is a good reason to avoid indiscriminate cairning, the cairns are so close together that any confusion should not be too serious.

Careful navigation is required on the descent over irregular broken ground from Letterbreckaun. To keep on the ridge, head first north-east for a few hundred yards and then north-west for a similar distance. When two tiny lochans are seen, one perched directly above the other, look for a point where a direct descent

The start of the climb

west into a narrow river valley can be made by taking a gully between crags.

That done, the remainder of the walk is easy. Take either bank downstream (but note that you must end up on the L bank), past a delightful little waterfall. Next note the stone walls and ruin ahead. Keep to their L and cross a fence, an extension L of the wall, at an easy point. Turn half-L to reach the Western Way, at this point a wide track but one which blends chameleon-like into the surrounding bogland, so that an act of faith — and a compass

Opposite: The descent route

— may be needed to follow it along the foot of the Maamturks close on the L. After 1¼ miles (2 km) on the Western Way, forest and a few houses heave into sight. Continue on beyond them, following roughly the electricity poles should the Way be unclear. When the Way reaches a metalled road turn R and walk back to the car-park.

1   *The Pilgrimage to Mamean*
This pilgrimage takes place in early August each year. The ceremonies connected with it take place at Mamean, a mountain pass 5 miles (8 km) from here. Once a place of pagan worship, it was later Christianized, and later still 'enlivened' by the addition of poteen-drinking and faction-fighting. The pilgrimage was revived recently and now has a more decorous format.

2   *The Western Way*
At present this Long Distance Route runs from Oughterard in County Galway west and north to Westport in Mayo, taking in some of the most spectacular scenery in the two counties. There are plans to extend it northwards from Westport. The route is not waymarked at present.

3   *The Maamturks Walk*
This marathon walk, which takes place in May each year, is reputed to be the toughest in Ireland. It passes south-east to north-west by Mam Ochoige. Fifteen miles (24 km) long with a climb of 8000 ft (2430 m), it takes in the entire length of the Maamturks from the Maam Cross-Maam Bridge road to Leenane. The descents and re-ascents from the five major passes, of which Mam Ochoige is one, make it particularly arduous. The record for the walk is about 5 hours, nearly half Naismith Rule's reckoning and this does not allow any time for stops.

3·16

MWEELREA

At 2686 ft (814 m) Mweelrea (pronounced *'Mweel-ray'*) is the highest peak in the West. Perhaps peak is not quite the right word: Mweelrea is, rather, the highest point of a massif, an undulating grassy area whose eastern side is abruptly terminated by a gigantic and magnificent corrie — one of several which has eaten into the massif. It is along the corrie edge that the other high points of the massif rise, 'half-peaks' with innocent grassy slopes on one side and the wicked plunging wall of the corrie on the other. The route's focal point is this corrie, but it also pays its respects to Mweelrea itself on the far end of the plateau, from which the views are stunning.

SAFETY NOTE

Two routes are described to the massif. If you suffer from vertigo or wish to avoid some airy scrambling, take the easier one.

ROUTE DESCRIPTION (Map 3.16)

If there is good visibility it might be helpful to study the route before starting — most of it can be seen from the road. The *difficult* route climbs directly up the northern (R) arm of the huge corrie on the opposite side of Doo Lough, ascends a small subsidiary peak, from your standpoint well below the skyline, and then advances directly up to the summit plateau. The *easy* route climbs the back wall of the corrie on a grassy ramp rising L to R to a low point on the summit plateau. Here the routes converge for the final ascent.

The difficult route Cross the stream flowing into Doo Lough using stepping-stones near the lough, cross the fence beyond and advance across the bog where, in dry weather, sundews *(1)* are particularly evident. As you climb along the inner side of the arm, watch out for a solitary rowan tree and take a narrow gully 20 yards (18 m) or so to its R. If this causes vertigo, retreat forthwith to the easy variation. A little further up, the summit

STARTING AND
FINISHING POINT
On the R335/L100
(Glenanane to
Louisburgh road)
just north of Doo
Lough (830694),
where there is
ample parking on
the roadside. From
Leenane turn L off
the N59 or from
Westport turn R
off the N59 onto
the R335, and park
8 miles (13 km)
beyond this turn at
the far end of Doo
Lough.

MAP
OS 1:50 000
Sheet 37.

LENGTH
10 miles (16 km)

ASCENT
3400 ft (1030 m)

plateau appears — bands of gently dipping sandstone strata with no evident way of breaching the ramparts they form.

Undeterred, climb the small peak mentioned above, and head for the rocky nose beyond, where the crux of the route awaits. Keep first to the L of the nose along a faint but reassuring path, scramble up the airy staircase, and then make a frontal scramble through rocks which ends in an easily climbed arête. Above this is the grass of the summit plateau.

The easy route Follow the difficult route to the sundews. Then follow the stream that runs into the north-west corner of Doo Lough. This leads into a valley where you can find your way over, or circumvent, low cliffs. Above the cliffs, ascend the grassy ramp and at its top climb an easy gully L to the lowest point in the corrie rim. Turn R (north-east) to reach the grassy plateau. Here the two routes converge.

From the plateau, walk to Benbury (2610 ft/795 m), which rises none too ostentatiously a few hundred yards further to the north-west, after which head to Mweelrea (2686 ft/814 m) over

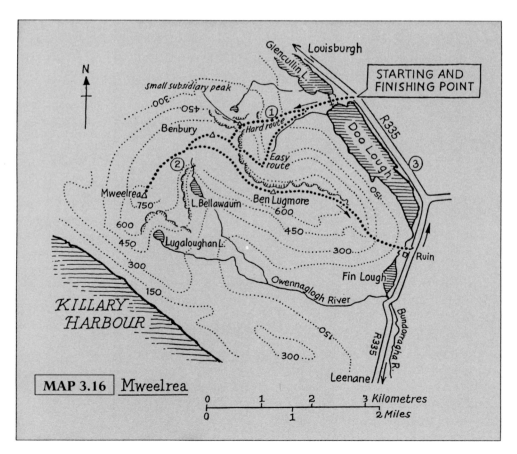

MAP 3.16 Mweelrea

DOOLOUGH TRAGEDY
1849
ERECTED TO THE MEMORY OF
THOSE WHO DIED IN
THE FAMINE OF 1845-49

*The Doo Lough
Tragedy memorial*

catastrophically sparse grass *(2)*. The summit area of Mweelrea is undistinguished, but as a viewpoint it is unsurpassed. Killary Harbour winds its sinuous way close at hand, beyond which crowd the Benchoonas, the Twelve Bens and the Maamturks. The Sheffry Hills and Ben Gorm rise to the east. Northwards is bog and fringing the sea the magnificent beach at Killadoon. Beyond it to the west a scattering of islands ride the ocean.

Return along the ascent route, bypassing Benbury, to reach the main corrie edge at its lowest point once more. A dramatic jagged skyline lies ahead. Note here, to the L of the giant 'tooth' rearing skyward, the flat-topped peak Ben Lugmore (2616 ft/803 m). Following the route from this point is child's play. Keep the corrie's rim on the L on a roller-coaster progress, veering R onto grassy slopes where rock formations bar the way.

At Ben Lugmore, take care not to follow the grassy spur

south-east; instead swing L to keep close to the corrie rim, here not quite so impressive. Continue steeply downhill, forking L over rocky ground onto the higher branch where the spur divides.

The steep and punishing descent resumes after the rocky ground. As you near the road (it is of course the R335 again) watch out for a ruin between it and the Bundorragha River. Ford the river here (alas, wet feet may be unavoidable) to gain the road, turn L and walk back to the starting point. On this walk look out on the R for the plaque to the victims of the Doo Lough tragedy in 1849 (3).

1   *The Sundew*

The sundew is a typical plant of the bogs and is easily recognizable because of the bright red splashes that its leaves impart to the otherwise dull-coloured stretches of bog. It makes up for the lack of minerals in its environment by the simple process of catching mineral-rich insects. This it does by trapping unlucky insects on its sticky tentacles and then dissolving and absorbing them.

2   *Erosion on the Hilltops*

This area has suffered greatly from over-grazing by sheep, caused by the EC Common Agricultural Policy which gives grants on the basis of the number of ewes run by each farmer, so that it is in each farmer's interest to run the maximum. The result is the erosion evident here.

3   *Tragedy at Doo Lough*

In 1849, towards the end of the Great Famine, a comparatively small and little-known, yet significant tragedy occurred hereabouts. A group of starving people who were trying to seek refuge in the workhouse at Louisburgh were advised to present themselves in person to the Guardians of the Workhouse at Delphi, 12 miles (19 km) away over rough tracks. The Guardians could — or would — do nothing for them, so the starving people had to return through the cold of an early spring. Some of them died on the way back. While the numbers involved are disputed, the main facts and therefore the poignancy of the incident is not. This event is remembered in a simple plaque on the side of the road here.

Mweelrea: the eastern side

THE GLENCOAGHAN
HORSESHOE

STARTING AND
FINISHING POINT
Ben Lettery Youth
Hostel (777483) on
the N59, 6 miles
(9.5 km) west of
Recess and 8 miles
(13 km) east of
Clifden. The Hostel
is on the northern
side of the road.
There is plenty of
space for safe
parking. Two miles
(3 km) of tedious
walking can be
avoided if two cars
are used, the
second leaving the
walkers about 1
mile (1.6 km) along
the track described
in the first para-
graph of the route
description. Here
there is room for
careful parking on
the verge.

MAPS
The 1:50 000
Connemara map is
recommended.

LENGTH
10 miles (16 km)

ASCENT
5200 feet (1590 m)

This is a classic among Irish hill walks, a demanding circuit taking in six of the rearing Twelve Bens in a lofty route over steeply rising and dipping terrain. It is the bare quartzite rock that distinguishes the walk from nearly all others in Ireland, and which gives it its unique character. The views all along the route are excellent: primarily the ever-changing vista of the Bens themselves into whose deepest recesses this walk penetrates. But that is not all: the Maamturks lie just across the Inagh Valley, and between Bens and Maamturks and curving round in a great arc to the south (thus blocking off the Bens from the watery bogland further south) runs a long, narrow line of interconnected lakes.

SAFETY NOTE
Although the total distance walked is modest, there is a lot of climbing and the descents can be just as tiring as the ascents. Be prepared for a long, energetic day.

ROUTE DESCRIPTION (Map 4.17)

With the Hostel on the L walk along the N59 for 1 mile (1.6 km), turning first L here onto a track. This track must constitute one of the most untidy and unprepossessing starts of any walk: 'temporary' caravan dwellings, straggling fences and rough ground combine to deter the sensitive walker. But persevere; after about 1 mile (1.6 km) of undulating progress, the full view of the circuit broken only by the curious snout pushing east of Benbreen/Binn Bhraoin comes fully into view. It is a magnificent sweep of peaks from Derryclare/Binn Dhoir Chlair nearby on the R to Ben Lettery/Binn Leitri on the L, vegetation climbing the lower slopes, glistening quartzite above to the very summits.

Choose any convenient point along here to leave the track and head half R for Derryclare (2220 ft/677 m) which rises steeply close at hand. Initially, the ground is rough and boggy, but it improves if a grassy ramp higher up, not essential for route-finding, is found. There is a long, unrelenting ·climb to the

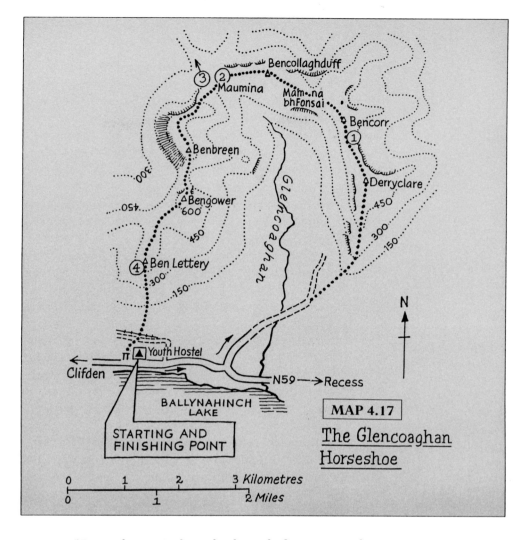

MAP 4.17

The Glencoaghan Horseshoe

summit of Derryclare, which marks the end of vegetation; from here on, the route is predominantly over rock all the way to Ben Lettery. A short drop and rather longer rise *(1)* ends in Bencorr/ Binn Chorr (2336 ft/712 m) where the views to Lough Inagh, and beyond that to the Maamturks, catch the eye.

Take the ridge of rock slabs heading initially north-west from Bencorr and drop to the pass at Mam na bhFonsai, taking care not to follow the formidable range running north-east that ends overlooking Lough Inagh. From the pass, climb sharply to Bencollaghduff/Binn Dhubh (2260 ft/698 m), a magnificent belvedere in the centre of the Bens, and commanding especially good views of the white cone of Benbaun/Binn Bhan, at 2395 ft (730 m) the highest of all the Bens.

Another steep drop, partly over narrow but safe ground, follows to Maumina/Mam Eidheach, a narrow, comparatively low pass (1476 ft/450 m), which is generally considered to be the centre around which the peaks of the Bens converge (2). Three valleys meet, or rather nearly meet here: the partly wooded valley of the Owenglin river running west, the unwooded part of which is in the Connemara National Park (3); Glencoaghan to the south; and Gleninagh/Gleann Eidhneach, not visible from here but only a little way off to the north-east. Between these three the highest pyramids of the Bens soar skywards, bare and awe-inspiring. Would it be an earthward descent into bathos to mention also that Maumina is an excellent place for a rest and a snack?

There is another steep climb with some avoidable scrambling to Benbreen/Binn Bhraoin (2276 ft/694 m), a difficult peak on which to navigate in bad weather. The initial climb ends in a rock-strewn plateau and a dog-leg L on it brings you to the summit cairn on the far end. If in doubt note that the eastern spur of Benbreen which projects unmistakably into the main valley is directly opposite the summit.

A steep scree descent, partly (but only partly) avoidable ends at another narrow pass. From here Bengower/Binn Gabhar (2184 ft/666 m) is due south. Once again and unsurprisingly, another steep ascent to the summit (you will surely be used to them by now!), this one involving some scrambling, though this is neither difficult nor vertigo-inducing.

South of Bengower, grass once again begins to predominate. Ben Lettery (1904 ft/580 m) (4) is but a short stroll away, but take care on this stretch *not* to follow the spur R towards Benglenisky/Binn Ghleann Uisce. Descend south of Ben Lettery towards the Hostel and the road through steep, rough wet vegetation. As you descend, the Hostel, partly obscured by clumps of trees, comes into view, and as is usual on difficult, lengthy descents at the end of a tiring day, seems to get no whit more prominent as you walk.

At length you will see a ruin ahead. Head for this, crossing the fence just before it (look for the place where the wires are bent to facilitate walkers). Cross the track ahead and near the Hostel go to the R side to use the stile at the boundary fence. Take the driveway to the road.

1   *The Patient Surveyor*
The remains of a stone shelter just above the col towards Bencorr was occupied by an OS surveyor in the 1840s when the major triangulation of Ireland was being carried out. He had to wait 7 weeks to get a clear day to see what he called the 'Kerry Man' on Carrauntoohil 90 miles (145 km) away.

Opposite: *The eastern end of the Bens*

92

2 *Muckanaght, the Green Hill*
From Maumina the peak of Muckanaght/Meacanach to the north-west may be seen. It is more rounded and greener than its neighbours, the reason being that alone among the Bens it is formed of schists, not quartzite. The schist breaks down easier than the quartzite, thus giving a gentler outline and forming better soil, which allows some grass to cling to its sides.

3 *The Connemara National Park*
The Connemara National Park takes in the near sides (only) of the three summits north and west of here as well as the summit of Bencullagh/An Chailleach and the area around it to the west. The Park stretches to the outskirts of Letterfrack, $5\frac{1}{2}$ miles (9 km) away. In all it covers 5000 acres (2000 hectares), mostly mountain but also with some areas of bog, heaths and grassland. The Visitor Centre at Letterfrack, which is open from Easter to the end of September, provides an audio-visual display, a stunning photographic display of Connemara scenery (though not as stunning as the display you should be experiencing here at Maumina), and picnic tables with the free use of electric kettles to brew your own hot drinks (the latter are not free). The Visitor Centre is a good excursion for a wet day.

4 *Caesar Otway on Ben Lettery*
Mr Caesar Otway, whom we last met on Muckish, also climbed Ben Lettery, which he found 'extremely rugged and precipitous'. He had a different type of anguish on Lettery to that which he experienced on Muckish. 'Some of our party', he thundered, 'called for the provision basket. It was little short of treason against the majesty of nature, to fix those eyes on rolls and cold beef, which ought to have been directed to one of the noblest views of Cunnemarra.'

It is more than likely that eating and viewing simultaneously would have compounded the affront.

The view across
Glencoaghan

INTRODUCTION

The mountains of the South-West, in effect the mountains of County Kerry since the contiguous hill area of west Cork is but a small adjunct, boast nearly all the highest mountains in Ireland, including all but two of its Munros. This paramount but simple fact does not itself make the mountains of Kerry attractive or challenging, but nevertheless they are. Tall (as small) *is* beautiful.

This is an area where the sea, and its numerous inlets, are never far away. The mountains are located on five peninsulas, five rugged fingers reaching westward into the ocean and separated by long, tapering bays — in geological terms drowned valleys. In many mountain areas the sea is ever-present, a deep blue plain stretching to the misty horizon. In others it reveals itself on the climb: sections of what appear first as disjointed lakes coalesce with height to be seen eventually as long inlets of the sea.

The other common feature of the South-West is the relative abundance of vegetation. The area benefits from the warmth of the Gulf Stream and so is characterized by exceptionally mild winters, especially in its southernmost reaches. In particular the area round Glengarriff in the far south is a humid hothouse of vegetation, so that the frequent epithet 'sub-tropical' that is applied to the region is not altogether an exaggeration.

The long inlets and rugged terrain mean that access is not easy in the South-West. Roads hug the coast and cross the peninsulas only by means of tortuous, sinuous passes. Add to that the perennial poor state of the roads so that the rule must be: leave yourself plenty of time for travel; you will probably need it.

In an area of splendid mountains some of the routes were 'musts'. The Coomloughra horseshoe simply had to be included. How could any mountaineering writer omit a circuit which encompasses the *three* highest peaks in Ireland and by far its most spectacular ridge walk? Brandon was in the same category: a great massif on the Dingle Peninsula, a superb juxtaposition of magnificent corrie, rugged hillside and rolling ocean — and a formidable Munro to boot.

Some of the others were not so obvious; one at least was chosen because it was characteristic of its area. The Beara

Peninsula is an area of lush vegetation, highly characteristic sandstone rock formations, but dull uplands and it was no easy matter to pick the best route. Nonetheless the Cummeengeera horseshoe is difficult to better.

A Paternoster lake on Brandon

One route which is easily accessible from Killarney is

Bennaunmore, a purely serendipitous discovery: on the map unpromising hilly area first chosen to while away a day of low cloud. However, a pleasant surprise was in store: regions far greater in extent and several times as high cannot boast a terrain as varied and as mountainously rugged, where each few steps reveal fresh delights.

The other two routes have connotations other than purely mountaineering ones. Mount Eagle is as much a cultural as a physical journey. At the remote end of the Dingle Peninsula it gives not only a highly scenic coastal walk, but also a glimpse into the remnants of Gaelic Ireland, the archaeological and linguistic remains of a once-rich culture now on a life-support system. Lastly, Gougane Barra, which has religious associations as well as cultural ones, is undoubtedly the finest area for walking in West Cork, both because of the dramatic views it gives of the corrie on which the route centres and the wide panorama it allows.

2·18

MOUNT EAGLE

For much of this walk the eye is drawn irresistibly towards the sea, and especially towards the islands which lie scattered over it. Pre-eminent is Great Blasket, a basking whale of a rock just off the pointing finger of Dunmore Head. Beyond it float the other islands of the Blaskets: Inishtooskert, Tearaght, Inishnabro and Inishvickillane — all of them carrying almost mystic significance for the last phase of Gaelic-speaking Ireland. Further away to the south rise the unmistakable Great and Little Skelligs, like the summits of jagged peaks rising sheer out of the ocean. Add to all this splendid views of the mountains of two peninsulas and the result is an easy yet rewarding walk of excellent and varied views.

ROUTE DESCRIPTION (Map 2.18)

With the car-park on the R walk 300 yards (270 m) south along the road and turn L at the 'walking-man' sign to go through a gate. Turn R immediately and follow the wall in which the gate is set, first parallel to the main road and then steeply uphill. Pass another 'walking-man' on your L *(1), (2)*, still following the wall. Where the wall turns sharply R continue straight ahead uphill along an intermittent wall and earth bank which constitutes a boundary line.

This boundary line can be easily followed all the way to the top of Mount Eagle: first fairly steeply uphill, then over rocks and steep ground at Beenacouma (1395 ft/425 m), where it almost disappears, and finally over grass on the nearly level stretch near the summit (1696 ft, 516 m), which is marked by an OS obelisk.

From the summit, head towards the corrie that holds Mt Eagle Lough to pick up the end of a green track. Walk north along it, with the cliff and lough to the R, continuing straight ahead where a branch on the R heads down the northern side of the corrie.

Follow the track all the way to the Dunquin–Kildurrihy road, turn R here and again L at the T-junction, which has three signposts, all pointing to Daingean (Gaelic for Dingle). And you

STARTING AND
FINISHING POINT
In the car-park on the seaward side of the R559 just south of the village of Coumeenoole (317976).

MAP
OS 1:50 000
Sheet 70.

LENGTH
7 miles (10 km)

ASCENT
1700 ft (530 m)

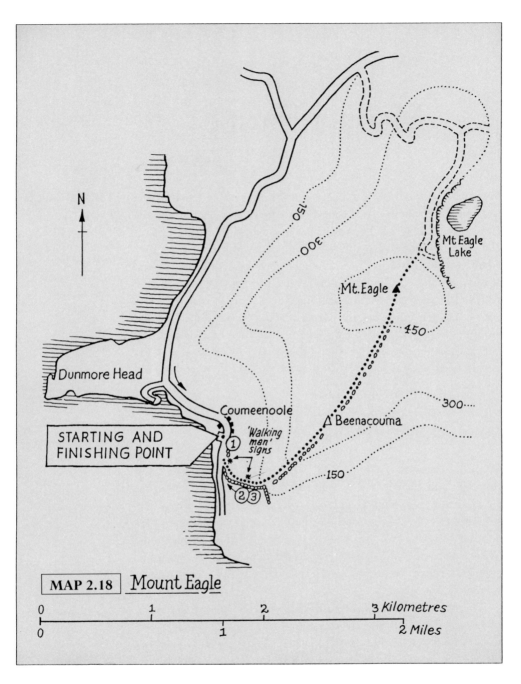

MAP 2.18 Mount Eagle

thought all roads led to Rome! Keep on this road, crossing the base of Dunmore Head *(3)*, to reach the car-park.

1 *The Slea Head Road*

The road on which this walk starts was built in the second half of the nineteenth century to relieve unemployment. This type of civil work, some of it of negligible practical use,

100

was the usual palliative to relieve a problem which has never *Slea Head from Ventry*
been satisfactorily solved except by the expedient of emi-
gration.

2   *The Blaskets*
The Great Blasket Island was inhabited until 1953, wholly by
Gaelic speakers. In that year the remaining inhabitants were
evacuated. There was a fine tradition of writing among the
islanders, the best known of whom, Peig Sayers, is buried in
the graveyard close to the end of the walk.

3   *Aftermath of the Armada*
A Spanish ship foundered in Blasket Sound between Dunmore Head and Great Blasket in September 1588 after the
disastrous rout of the Armada. Hundreds of Spanish were
drowned and only one, the pilot's son, was saved and he was
captured. A Spanish prince who was among those lost is
buried in the old burial ground at Dunquin.

Gougane Barra

STARTING AND
FINISHING POINT
Opposite the
church at Gougane
Barra (091657),
where there is
ample parking.
Gougane Barra is
off the R584/T64
(Macroom-Bally-
lickey road) on the
R travelling from
Macroom. It is well
signposted.

MAPS
OS half-inch to the
mile Sheet 24
inadequately covers
the route. Sheet 21
covers the area just
north of the route
and is useful for
identifying features
beyond Sheet 24.

LENGTH
7 miles (11 km)

ASCENT
1750 ft (530 m)

Gougane Barra (pronounced *Goo-gawn Barra*) is the jewel in the crown of the Shehy mountains of West Cork. The curious name properly refers to the narrow lake whose only major island contains a tiny picturesque church surrounded by trees. West of the lake a long, partly wooded corrie indented by several side valleys is cut into the plateau of the Shehy mountains. The walk circumscribes this corrie in a wide, clockwise sweep. With no real summits to be climbed, the walk's interest centres on the views of the lake and corrie, but more so outwards to the Paps, the great corrie of Lough Nambrackderg and the further-off jagged outline of the Reeks.

SAFETY NOTE

This is a moderately short walk with what should be a simple navigational objective: to keep the corrie on the R. However, there are few significant landmarks – the 'peaks' barely rise above the plateau so in bad visibility you should use the small landmarks, primarily the lochans, to determine your position. There are only a few places where a direct descent to the valley floor can be attempted.

ROUTE DESCRIPTION (Map 2.19)

With the car-park on the L *(1)* walk along the road for 80 yards (70 m), turning L here through a gate and up a minor track at a toilet disguised as a circular African straw-hut. Follow the track uphill until it resolutely heads south-east, clearly the wrong direction. Strike diagonally R uphill here, cross a fence, and then aim for a rocky pinnacle high above. Not a peak, this is nonetheless a clear landmark. Its name, Foilastookeen, means 'The cliff of the little pinnacle' and this is a good description.

From here the next target is the unnamed peak close by to the south-west where a fence is visible on the skyline. Around this peak the views open up outwards from Gougane Barra corrie; Bantry Bay and the aptly named voluptuous Paps being conspicuous. Keeping the fence on the L follow it over rough ground past three small lakes on the L. At the last of these lakes (where the fence ends) a grid bearing of 350° will be needed to find Lough Glas high on the plateau to the north-west.

From Lough Glas continue slightly downwards to the head of a gully R *(2)*, crossing a fence close to it to reach a lochan. At this point the immense corrie of Lough Nambrackderg with a long, narrow waterfall plunging into it, can be seen at its finest. Continue across wet bogland to Bealick (1764 ft/538 m), the only 'peak' on this route to have a cairn of any sort. Given the number of hillocks hereabouts it is a useful construction.

The walk would appear to be almost over, with only a descent R to the start. Not so. The cliffs overlooking Gougane Barra Lake are low but dangerous, and though they can be circumvented the safe routes are easier to find in retrospect. Keep therefore to the shoulder north-east from Bealick, walking to a small lake set in quaking bog and continue straight ahead beyond it, dropping off the L side of the nose facing the Owenashrone River. Turn R at the river and follow the L bank down through tussocky country to a small copse of conifers where the river swings R. Cross wet bogland here to a narrow metalled road *(3)*, turn R along it and L at the foot of the hill (R leads to the nearby substantial farmhouse). At the main road turn R for the starting point.

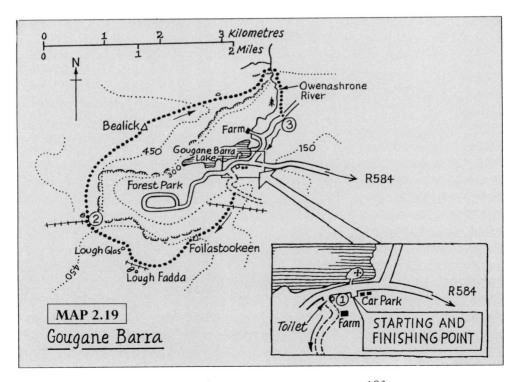

MAP 2.19
Gougane Barra

The Church at
Gougane Barra

1 *The Church at Gougane Barra*
The small church on Holy Island opposite the car-park, which can be reached by a causeway, dates from as recently as 1900 and was inspired by a chapel on the Rock of Cashel. The stone court nearby dates from the end of the seventeenth century. The wooden cross in the centre of the court is inscribed in Latin, English and Gaelic: 'here stood in the sixth century, the cell of St Finbar, first bishop of Cork'. St Finbar had a monastery here which, being constructed of simple perishable material, has long since disappeared.

2 *The Fortuitous Gully*
This gully played a happy role for Irish insurgents in May 1921 when rebel troops were hemmed in on all sides by superior British forces. Helped by local guides the rebels retreated into Gougane Barra, and at night, led by a local guide, they climbed a long rope up this gully and thus escaped into Kerry.

3 *The Pilgrim's Road*

Opposite: *Gougane*
Barra lake

This road marks the end of the pilgrims' route into Gougane Barra, the start of which is noted in Route 20.

2·20

BENNAUNMORE

STARTING AND
FINISHING POINT
At the end of the
side-road running
along the eastern
side of the Lough
Guitane (034839).
From Killarney take
the N71 (Kenmare
road) turning L at
the signpost 'Lough
Guitane 2½', which
is just after the jar-
veys' gathering-
point about 2½
miles (4 km) from
Killarney. Drive
straight ahead for
4 miles (6.4 km),
turning R onto a
gated road here.
Drive for a further
1.4 miles (2.2 km)
and park on open
ground near a
bridge which serves
a farmhouse.

MAP
OS 1:50 000 Sheet
79.

LENGTH
6½ miles
(10.5 km)

ASCENT
1650 ft (500 m)

The area south-east of Killarney close to Lough Guitane is ideal
for leisurely free-range exploration. The discriminating walker
can enjoy narrow but deep glens, low but soaring peaks flanked
by impressive cliffs, ancient oakwoods and tiny hidden lakes, all
in a virtually unfrequented area within a couple of miles of Bennaunmore, a peak of volcanic rock. The route given here is a
suggestion only, a vehicle to point to the small-scale hidden
delights of the area. Take into account the few cautions given
below and you can wander around safely as the fancy takes you.
Give yourself plenty of time: much of the terrain is difficult —
and all of it repays leisurely pottering.

ROUTE DESCRIPTION (Map 2.20)

Follow the track south-east (that is, not over the bridge) past a
ruin on the L. Cross two minor streams, and just beyond the
second pass through a gate. This gate marks your entry into open
country and you should note carefully its position since you will
have to find it on the return.

From the gate head south-east (exactly 120° grid) towards a
tiny valley visible from here. Walk up the valley (1). ('Walk' is a
euphemism for struggle: crossing from one bank to the other and
back again, clambering over rocks, climbing through high vegetation, and even stone-hopping up the stream when all else
fails.) After at least a half-hour's work with little progress to
show for it, you will gain a tiny basin with a hill beyond flanked
by two valleys, that to the R sheltering a small copse of oaks.
Follow this valley, which gives unexpectedly easy going over
long grass, up to a grassy col. Lough Nabroda comes suddenly
into view below, and the rocky cliffs on the eastern flank of
Bennaunmore (2) come equally suddenly into view ahead. A good
spot to rest after your strenuous efforts.

Walk down to the near side of the lake to pick up a path
running beside it on its L-hand side. Follow the path to the end of
the lake, where it disappears, leaving the walker to face the wet

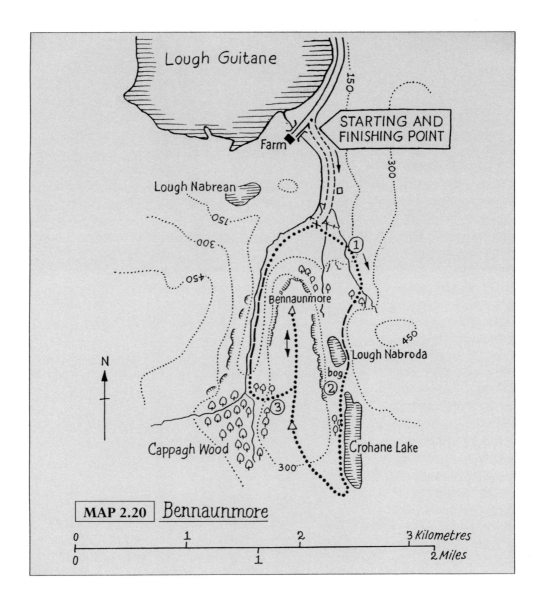

MAP 2.20 Bennaunmore

Lough Guitane

150

STARTING AND
FINISHING POINT

Farm

300

Lough Nabrean

150

300

450

Bennaunmore

450

Lough Nabroda

bog

②

Crohane Lake

N

①

③

Cappagh Wood

300

0   1   2   3 Kilometres

0   1   2 Miles

grassy bogland beyond to Lake Crohane alone. Here you have
a choice: a difficult route through a mixed wood on the west
(i.e. R) side or an easy route through grass and heather on the
east (i.e. L). Either way, the view of the Roughty River over the
brow of the hill at the southern end is worth a peep.

Next, Bennaunmore (1490 ft/454 m). The south top is easily
climbed directly from the far south end of Lake Crohane over
rough open country. The north top is a there-and-back to the
saddle between it and the south top, but is worth the effort for
the views it gives of Lough Guitane and the high plateau of

Bennaunmore from near the start

Mangerton to the west. At the saddle once again descend carefully west into Cappagh Glen *(3)*. This is a steep slope through an ancient 'petrified' wood of oak, holly and birch whose recumbent branches are not for grasping trustingly — they are all too liable to break off in rotten fragments in the hand. Incidentally, the descent directly from Lake Crohane into the south of Cappagh Glen is not recommended: this slope is even more hazardous than the one described.

On the valley floor turn R (north) to walk by a stream on its R-hand bank. This leads to an impressive natural amphitheatre a little way on, the walls especially high on Bennaunmore's flank to the R and a clear indication that a descent anywhere from Bennaunmore's west flank would be suicidal. At this point the amphitheatre looks exitless: luckily the stream has found a narrow but easy passage, so simply follow it along a clear path.

Beyond the exit follow the burgeoning stream into an alluvial plain of short grass and after a distinct bend to the R veer away from it to gain the gate crossed earlier in the day (the fence ahead will halt onward progress anyway). Take the track beyond, the initial track of the day, directly to the car.

1   *The Old Pilgrim Road*
    The stone uprights occasionally seen along here are the remains of an old pilgrim road which led from the plains of Kerry north of here across the mountains to Goùgane Barra in west Cork. The pilgrims gathered there for the festival of St Finbar on the last Sunday in September. We have already met the other end of this route in Route 19.

2   *The Giant's Causeway of Kerry*   *Lough Nabroda*

The volcanic columnar cliffs of Bennaunmore range for about a $\frac{1}{4}$ mile (0.4 km) and in places are about 200 ft (60 m) high. Only some of the columns exhibit a regular polygonal cross-section. They are not safe for climbing as they come away easily from the cliff face. There is a stream flowing north from Lough Nabroda but it is underground, being blocked by fallen columns and scree from Bennaunmore.

3   *The Petrified Forest of Cappagh*

This forest, because of its remote location and difficult underfoot terrain survived the mass clearing of the native oak to make charcoal for iron-smelting furnaces in the seventeenth century. Many of the trees to the south are leafless, hence the term 'petrified'. 'Cappagh' (ceapach) is the Gaelic for 'decayed', indicating that the forest must have been in decline for many years.

2.21

THE CUMMEENGEERA HORSESHOE

STARTING AND
FINISHING POINT
On the road into
Cummeengeera
(760559). Drive to
Lauragh village,
around the junction
of the R571/L62
with the R574 (the
Healy Pass road).
Taking the initial
measurement from
this crossroads,
drive west, that is,
towards Castletown
Berehaven, for 0.8
miles (1.3 km).
Turn L here, sign-
posted 'Glanmore
Lake'. Turn R after
0.6 miles (1.0 km)
and drive for nearly
1 mile (1.4 km) to a
gated track on the
R beyond which is
a bungalow. There
is parking here or a
few hundred yards
further on.

MAP
OS Kerry District
one-inch to the
mile map.

LENGTH
6½ miles (10.5
km)

ASCENT
2450 ft (750 m)

'Benches' are a notable feature of this walk in the Beara Peninsula. The word 'benches' conjures up a smooth horizontal surface, but used by the locals this is a gross misnomer: the great sandstone slabs called 'benches' lie tilted at high, awkward angles and rise line upon line to form the hills, so that on the skyline they appear like the teeth of a huge circular saw. Along their grain walking is easy; a route crossing them is painfully slow.

The other remarkable feature of this area is the luxuriant vegetation in the lowlands: oakwoods drape themselves over the lower slopes and crowd around lakes; rhododendrons, ferns, mosses and a hundred species of flora thrive in the mild climate and high humidity. All quite memorable when viewed from above, but tortuous when traversed lower down.

ROUTE DESCRIPTION (Map 2.21)

Take the track on the R of the road through two gates, turning L off it before the first farmhouse. A tough climb (1), initially through bracken though along the grain of the benches, ensues to the top of Cumeennahillan (1183 ft/361 m), or rather the tops (there are several), one of which is graced by a few heaped stones masquerading as a cairn.

A short drop through wet, boggy country ends in a climb with the grain of the benches to Knocknaveachal (1685 ft/514 m) which has no cairn, but a jagged pinnacle acts as a satisfactory substitute. From here the convoluted folding of Tooth Mountain ahead can be seen to perfection, one fold uncannily like the imprint of the lower set of a giant's teeth (2).

A distinct, avoidable vertical slab is a reassuring landmark on the route to Tooth Mountain (1945 ft/593 m), the climb to which is short but difficult, through high slabs and along grassy ledges. The top is a tangle of rocky outcrops and puddles with no clear landmark to indicate position.

The terrain changes markedly after Tooth Mountain, slabs yielding to grassy bogland, thus allowing speedier progress. Coo-

110

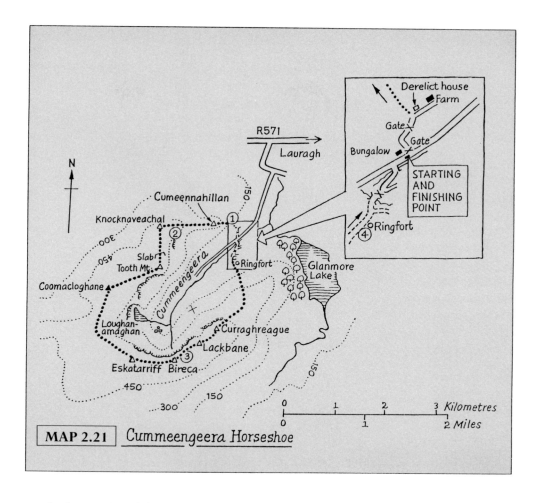

MAP 2.21 Cummeengeera Horseshoe

macloghane (1969 ft/600 m) is another indefinite top or rather would be were it not for its OS obelisk. After Coomacloghane, slabs re-appear intermittently as far as the peat-hagged plateau that lies along the Cork-Kerry border. Once on this plateau, swing L to keep to the edge of the steep ground at the head of Cummeengeera. Along here the great rocky bulk of Hungry Hill to the south-east dominates the skyline.

Walk along level ground to Eskatarriff (1973 ft/601 m), an unimpressive set of slabs, after which climb a small but steep pinnacle, unheralded on the maps. This is Bireca, its L flank dropping sheer into the inner recesses of Cummeengeera. The upper end of the valley visible from here is interesting. Separated from the lower end of Cummeengeera by a steep climb along a track, the valley is now deserted though it retains the traces of field boundaries and the remains of a house *(3)*, all of which from this lofty viewpoint appear as though on a map.

The next target is Lackbane (1984 ft/604 m), a stiff climb through rocky terrain. Beyond this, climb Curraghreague (1970 ft/600 m), its sister peak, which has a small cairn and whose north-west side drops far down into the glen in rock formations which look like organ pipes.

From Curraghreague make a steep descent over narrow ground offering excellent views of Lake Glanmore to the R and the lovely wooded lake and inlet country ahead. The drop ends at a narrow pass where the tempting direct descent L should not be attempted; it contains a wicked terrain of bracken and hidden boulder. Instead climb the hill directly ahead (it is only 100 ft/ 30 m or so) and descend north heading for the grassy circular mound below *(4)*. Take the path to its L, cross the area where it appears as if rhododendrons have been deliberately planted (surely not!) and carry on north to pick up a track.

Follow this across a bridge of rock slabs and through a gate. Beyond this turn L onto a better track at a hairpin bend (on the better track). Follow this track over a bridge to a metalled road and turn R for the starting point.

1   *Sub-tropical Gardens at Dereen*
     The woods of the Dereen Tropical Gardens just beyond Lauragh should be visible on the ascent. Built up over 130 years, the gardens flourish in the warm, damp climate. They include New Zealand ferns which although rare in the British Isles, thrive here; and giant conifers of north-west America, some of which are over 100 ft (30 m) tall.

2   *A Dental Mix-up at the Ordnance Survey*
     Knocknaveachal means 'the hill of the teeth' and the next mountain is called 'Tooth Mountain'. It seems that the English sappers got their nomenclature a little garbled when they were surveying in the nineteenth century. Considering this imprint the latter mountain seems the better candidate for the dental title.

3   *The Rabach*
     The ruined village in the upper reaches of Cummeengeera, which never had a road into it, illustrates the lengths to which people had to go to find a modicum of cultivatable land in pre-famine Ireland.
         There is a macabre story of a double murderer, Sean an Rabach, who dwelt here. He killed an Englishman, probably a deserter from a ship in Berehaven, and strangled a woman who found out about this crime. Many years later he was caught and hanged.

4   The Earth Ringfort
The ruined village in
This earth ringfort is one of the tens of thousands scattered all   *Cummeengeera*
over Ireland and dating from about 2000 BC to AD 500,
though some date from much later and a few were inhabited
until 1700. Homesteads were built within them and the fort
acted as a shelter from the wind, and a protection at night for
cattle against wolves, etc. They seldom had any direct
military significance.

3·22

THE COOMLOUGHRA HORSESHOE

STARTING AND
FINISHING POINT
At the junction of
the unclassified
road running along
the north-west side
of Lough Acoose
with that running
along the eastern
side (759859).
Assuming that one
is facing uphill on
the main street in
Killorglin take the
road signposted
Cappanalea on the
L of this street.
After 0.8 miles (1.3
km) fork R, also
signposted Cappa-
nalea, and continue
ahead for another
6.8 miles (10.9 km).
The exact parking
place is not critical.

MAPS
This walk is well
covered by a variety
of OS and other
maps. The
recommended map
is the OS 1:25 000
'The Macgilly-
cuddy's Reeks'.

LENGTH
6½ miles (10.5 km)

ASCENT
4050 ft (1240 m)

The sharp arête of the Beenkeragh Ridge is the finest in Ireland, falling in stretches sheer to the east and almost as steeply to the west. At its south stands Carrauntoohil (pronounced *Carawn-too-hill*) at 3414 ft (1039 m) the highest peak in Ireland; to its north is Beenkeragh, only 100 ft (29 m) lower and the second highest mountain. Beyond these proud and stately peaks the ridge sweeps in one direction to Skegmore and in the other to twin-peaked Caher (pronounced *Care*), the third highest. All these peaks and the fine ridges between them surround the hour-glass shaped lakes of Coomloughra and Eagher. This is by far the finest ridge walk in Ireland and many would say the most exhilarating and rewarding circuit.

SAFETY NOTE

The route, mostly a narrow ridge, is easy to negotiate navigationally, as the many cliffs in the area do not allow much latitude for error. If you suffer from *severe* vertigo do not attempt the ridge from Carrauntoohil to Beenkeragh (the 'Beenkeragh Ridge'), especially if the rocks are likely to be wet or if the winds are high. The walk is in an anti-clockwise direction: this allows the highest peak in Ireland, Carrauntoohil, to be climbed *before* the Beenkeragh Ridge, so that one will at least have had the satisfaction of achieving this if one has to retreat. An anti-clockwise circuit also means that the difficult stretch of the Beenkeragh Ridge (it is near Carrauntoohil) is tackled early on thus facilitating a return if necessary.

ROUTE DESCRIPTION (Map 3.22)

Walk a ½ mile (800 m) down the minor road along the eastern side of Lough Acoose, turning L off it opposite a prominent headland of Lough Acoose to cross rough, pathless ground and meet a fence and path parallel to it running along the north-west spur of Caher. Turn R here and follow the path and fence over good ground. Where the fence ends continue upwards still on a clear path through a boulder field to attain the first of the two

114

The Beenkeragh Ridge from Caher

peaks on Caher, which inexplicably has two adjacent cairns. The main top, which has to make do with one cairn, is a little farther on. At 3200 ft (1001 m) it predictably commands marvellous views. Cliffs fall steeply L into Coomloughra, Carrauntoohil rises ahead and to its L the jagged Beenkeragh Ridge terminates in the great rocky mound of Beenkeragh. Among the many peaks to the west the pyramid of Mullaghanattin is the most prominent.

Still on a clear path follow the narrow ridge east of Caher. From the col towards Carrauntoohil take the broad boulder-strewn ridge to the summit itself by-passing, near the summit, the Beenkeragh Ridge on the L. On this ascent, note the long ridge running east. This is the eastern section of the Reeks *(1)*, a fine arc of mountains which boasts no fewer than three or five Munros (it depends what is considered a Munro as there is not much of a drop between some of them).

Carrauntoohil (3414 ft/1039 m) is crowned by an ugly cross, a cairn and an OS obelisk *(2)*. Its summit stands as a promontory squarely facing north, looking over the plains of Kerry beyond the Hag's Glen. The views encompass much of what has already been described on the ascent and so need not be repeated. Among the many mountain features visible the formidable, steeper side of the Beenkeragh Ridge undulating jaggedly near at hand must attract what is hoped is a not too nervous eye.

So to the Ridge. Retrace your steps to the south-west for 100 yards (90 m), and then descend directly and steeply to the Ridge,

115

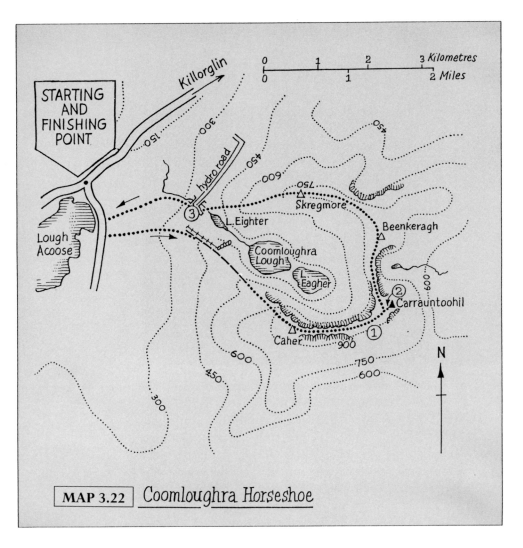

MAP 3.22 Coomloughra Horseshoe

which runs initially north-west (*Important: it is suicidal to attempt to walk directly to the Ridge from the summit of Carrauntoohil*). Once on the Ridge the crux, a rocky gendarme, comes early. The vertigo-free will clamber over the airy summit, the rest will scramble ignominiously lower down on the L. After this, the rest of the Ridge can be enjoyed as there is nothing half so scaring ahead. Now that *some* relaxation is possible (but not too much, carelessness can still easily result in disaster), watch out particularly for the Hag's Teeth far down on the R, great prongs of rock in the glen of the same name.

Beenkeragh, 3314 ft (1010 m), is reached after a short, steep, rocky ascent. The views are magnificent, especially back towards Carrauntoohil. After Beenkeragh take the ridge heading north-west (not the one north-east) towards Skregmore (2790 ft/ 851 m) and if this is done correctly, navigation thereafter is simple; the ground, steep on both sides, is ample warning against carelessness and the only possible error is the gross one of wandering down the subsidiary ridge towards Skregbeg.

Skregmore is, for the theoretically minded anyway, a problem. The five tops are difficult to distinguish, having only three cairns between them. For the record, the third of these tops, the one from which a ridge heads to Skregbeg, is the highest. Skregbeg is useful to the academics for determining exact positions — while the rest of us get on with the job of climbing all the tops.

There is likely to be no mistake about the descent from the 'fifth' Skregmore: its steepness has an air of finality. From its foot, head for the mouth of the long narrow Lough Eighter (not to be confused with Lough Eagher to the east). Take the rough road *(3)* at the mouth for the short distance to the bridge, and leave it here to follow the L bank of the river downstream. After 500 yards (450 m) where the river bends sharply R, veer southwest over a boggy saddle between rocky outcrops. Beyond these, head to the R side of the prominent headland mentioned in the first paragraph of the route description to reach the road. Turn R for the starting point.

1   *The Reeks*

The Reeks (properly the Macgillicuddy's Reeks — so named after a former local landlord) stretches from the Gap of Dunloe and runs all the way to and including Skregmore. The Munros and Tops (doubtful Munros), starting at the Gap of Dunloe and working west, are: Cruach Mhor (3062 ft/ 932 m), an unnamed top, Knocknapeasta (3190 ft/988 m), an unnamed top, Cnoc an Chuillin (3141 ft/958 m), Carrauntoohil and Beenkeragh (3314 ft/1010 m). The Reeks Walk, an annual long distance walk starting at the northern end of the Gap of Dunloe, took in all the peaks to Carrauntoohil and ended at Lough Acoose. It was discontinued in recent years partly because of the erosion caused by too many walkers.

2   *Carrauntoohil*

At 3414 ft (1039 m) this is the highest mountain in Ireland, though only the third of the four highest mountains in each of the countries in the British Isles. The bicycle which unaccountably used to be suspended on a bar at the summit has equally unaccountably disappeared.

Isaac Weld, an early mountaineer writing in 1807, used only barometric observations estimated the height of the mountain at 3418 ft, a remarkably accurate figure. He gives a vivid account of a direct descent from the summit of

117

Lough Acoose and the Reeks

'Gheraun-tuel', one which cannot be recommended:
We were conducted to a precipice, at least sixty feet deep, down which we were told it was necessary to take our course. The proposal startled us, nor did we consider how it was practicable; but the guide seating himself at the brink of it, on a rock which presented an even surface nearly to the bottom of the precipice, slid down it, taking the precaution, however, to impede the velocity of the descent, by catching hold of the tufts of long grass which grew from the crevices at either side. His example was followed without hesitation.

3 *Hydro Scheme at Lough Eighter*
This scheme is funded as a Valorean EC project. It generates a minute amount of electricity in a country which already has an ample supply. The approach road, which is all too evident, is a brutal intrusion in an area of great beauty. Two pipes run from here: a 6-inch one for Killorglin water supply and an 18-inch one for the generation at Cottoner's River.

4.23

BRANDON

At least one Scotsman has declared Brandon to be the finest mountain in the British Isles. While the not-so-canny Hamish Brown may now regret what might have been a hasty, off-the-cuff-remark (let's be charitable to the disloyal Scot), Brandon is undoubtedly a superb mountain. Far out towards the western end of the Dingle Peninsula, its eastern side plunges in a series of corries and cliffs to Brandon Bay, to inert boglands and to the high Conor Pass. West and north it confronts the Atlantic in a sweep of sea-cliff broken by isolated coves. A unique delight is the chain of paternoster lakes, a dozen or so (it depends on what you count as a lake) perched one over the next. These are set into the long corrie which truncates the summits of both Brandon and Brandon Peak, its high southern extension. The route described is probably the finest traverse of the mountain, offering marvellous scenic views on a safe, not-too-long circuit with, unusually for this part of the world, a clear path at least as far as the summit.

ROUTE DESCRIPTION (Map 4.23)

With the church on the L, walk past a plaque to airmen lost in World War II (1), on the R of the village street. Turn L onto a side road after ½ mile (0.8 km) from the start (it is signposted 'Hillcrest'), walk uphill to the T-junction, turn L and at the upper end of a severe S-bend where the road ends at a farmhouse, follow two signposts encouragingly labelled 'Mt Brandon'. This is the start of the Pilgrims' Route.

The second signpost leads to a grotto near at hand from where a path, needlessly adorned with obtrusive red and white poles, leads gradually uphill with higher ground on the R. At a large cairn (the first) the views, up to this point dominated by Brandon Peak and only slowly varying, open up dramatically. The paternoster lakes (2) are revealed one by one, and as the path swings R it faces directly into the head of the corrie, cliffs rising jaggedly and menacingly in nearly all directions.

STARTING AND
FINISHING POINT
The church (on the
L) in the village of
Cloghnane (511114).
From Tralee take
the R559/T68 and
then the R560 following signs for
Brandon or Brandon Point. The village itself is rather
indifferently signposted, and to
make it worse the
Gaelic form
'Cloghan' is used in
places along the
road.

MAP
OS 1:50 000 Sheet
70.

LENGTH
11½ miles (18.5
km)

ASCENT
4000 ft (1210 m)

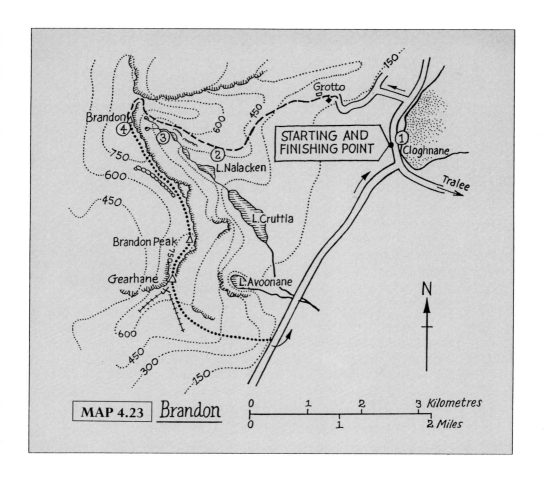

MAP 4.23 Brandon

Keeping to the path *(3)*, pass a lochan (four close together will be visible from higher up) and ascend the corrie wall on a steep but safe path. At the corrie top, turn L and with the sheer drop into the corrie L, walk 350 yards (320 m) to Brandon (3127 ft/952 m) *(4)*. The views from the summit are varied: dominated by the ocean to the north and west, and by plain and mountain in other directions. It is a wonderful panorama — when it can be seen — for Brandon is often cloud-topped, or as they say in the neighbourhood — 'it mostly wears its cap'

South of Brandon the path disappears, but no matter since all that is needed is to keep the corrie cliffs on the L and walk downhill (except for one short rise) all the way to the col towards Brandon Peak. In bad weather, the col may be recognized by a wall which meanders in from the R across the slope near the col, and abdicates to a line of stones at the col itself. South of the col climb steadily, cliffs still on the L, to cairned Brandon Peak (2764 ft/842 m).

120

From the Peak continue south on a gently undulating slope to Gearhane, a short narrow ridge about 2635 ft (803 m) high with steep grassy slopes on both sides. Walk down the gentle slope south of Gearhane on what is now a spur to an upland gate, flanked by fences at an unusually acute angle. Keep to the L of the fences and the gate so keeping close to the steep ground on the L.

Follow the spur as it swings L and gently descends, a descent which postpones and exacerbates the inevitable — a short but tough, steep descent through high heather. On this descent veer L to a sheep dip on the road to avoid new forestry directly below the nose. Gain the road at the dip and walk $2\frac{1}{2}$ miles (4 km) back

The Paternoster Lake

121

to the village, turning L at the outskirts of the village to reach the church.

1   *The Plaque in Cloghnane*

The plaque commemorates the Polish, British and German airmen who died in four separate plane crashes, all of which occurred in the area in the years 1940–43. One of the crashes occurred on the hill to the R of the Pilgrims' Route. Another crash in those years was that of a German fighter plane which landed with little damage. The crew set it on fire before it could be impounded.

2   *Paternoster Lakes*

The paternoster lakes are so called because the chain resembles the beads on a rosary, one of whose prayers is the 'Our Father' (*Pater Noster*). Some authorities claim that there are 16 lakes in the chain.

3   *St Patrick's Cabbage*

St Patrick's Cabbage (*Saxifraga spathularis*) grows freely in the rock crevices here. The flowers, which are open from May to July, are pink and white with crimson spots; the leaves grow in a basal rosette and are narrow towards the base. It is prolific among the mainly acid rocks of Cork and Kerry. London Pride is a hybrid of it.

4   *Brendan the Navigator*

The mountain is named after St Brendan the Navigator, who set sail from Brandon Creek near here in about the year 550 with a band of fellow monks, and who (apocryphally) discovered Greenland and even America. It is accepted that Iceland and probably Greenland were colonized from Ireland before the arrival of the Vikings, so the hagiography has some basis. The unimpressive mounds of stones on the summit are termed St Brendan's Well and Oratory.

In 1868 an amazing 20,000 people attended a mass here.

The Blaskets from Brandon

APPENDICES

ACCESS AND RIGHTS-OF-WAY FOR THE WALKER

Particularly in the Republic, but also in Northern Ireland, there is a great discrepancy between the strictly legal situation on rights-of-way and public access and the practical situation. *Legally*, in both jurisdictions hill-walkers have right of passage only in National Parks, on Long Distance Routes and in some state forests. In addition, in Northern Ireland there is a modest system of rights-of-way along the lines of those in England and Wales. In practice, however, in both jurisdictions the situation is much more favourable than this.

If a walker is in open (i.e., unenclosed) country he has little to fear and is much more likely to be exchanging greetings rather than trading insults with the farmers he encounters. In enclosed fields and near farmhouses it would be prudent to seek permission to cross land or walk through farm-yards, and it is unlikely that a polite request will be refused. In this context the closing off of commonage at present a minor but growing threat, makes access considerably harder.

Of course, the walker can expect a less than civil reception if he is not following the Country Code. To the farming community, the two most important items of this Code (but not the only ones) relate to dogs and fences.

Dogs must be under proper control, particularly in sheep country – and most of the uplands are sheep country. Walkers should never stand on fence wires; they may look the same afterwards but they are in fact irretrievably weakened. In a few places on these walks fences are to be crossed. However, there are gaps in most fences, and where there are not, there are always convenient rocks to facilitate a crossing.

Walkers enjoy this live-and-let-live attitude everywhere in the uplands. The only possible exception is Wicklow, which is so near a large city and its hordes of vandals that some farmers' tempers have understandably become somewhat frayed. The routes given in this book for Wicklow should not result in clashes. Elsewhere in Wicklow and, of course, in the contiguous mountains of County Dublin, one should be circumspect and heed notices.

It has to be admitted that, especially for visitors, this situation is not completely satisfactory. A visitor used to cast-iron rights-of-ways may, at least initially, feal uneasy in a country of goodwill but no guarantees. A few forays should improve their confidence; after all, it is supposed to be Ireland of the welcomes!

SAFETY

Safety is a dull topic – until an emergency when the effects of not taking safety measures will be suddenly and powerfully evident. Do not postpone sensible precautions until it is too late.

Of all the factors influencing safety, weather is the most important by far. The easiest route in bad weather can be far more hazardous than the hardest one in good weather. Cloud, wind and rain disorientate, weaken and chill, as well as drastically reducing your enjoyment. In cloud it is easy to veer by 180° in a few minutes when you think that you are walking straight ahead.

Other variables are the area and how well you know it, the number of people on the walk and their abilities, the quality of available maps, the time to darkness and the severity of the route. For instance, in good weather with a small, strong party, in an area you know well you can try a far more strenuous route than you would try if all these factors were unfavourable. In any event, an experienced party in bad or changeable weather should always consist of at least four people.

The route you walk and the precautions you take will depend on the variables listed above, always remembering that in Ireland the hills are likely to be unfrequented and a mountain rescue service may take a long time to reach the scene of an accident.

Before you set out, therefore, in a spirit of fine, careless rapture you should refer to the following checklist, all items of which should be carefully considered.

Before you go
Listen to the weather forecast.
Choose a route appropriate to your experience and the weather.
Leave a note of your intended route.

Take with you
A basic first aid kit, sufficient food and drink, proper clothing (especially boots) with some as spare, a small torch in winter, map and compass (the latter is particularly important in Ireland). Leave a change of clothing in your car.

On the walk
Keep an eye on deteriorating conditions and turn back if these warrant it – if you think you can just about make it, don't try.
Keep clear of cliffs, especially in high winds.

If an accident occurs
Keep calm. Keep the patient as warm and comfortable as possible and then go for help with a note of the injuries and the patient's exact position. Mountain rescue may be alerted, north or south, by ringing 999 and asking for mountain rescue.

Lastly, at all times take with you a few cells of commonsensical grey matter between your ears. They are your best guarantee against disaster.

GIVING A GRID REFERENCE

A grid reference is an excellent way of 'pinpointing' a feature, such as a church or mountain summit, and can be determined from all Ordnance Survey and most other maps mentioned in this book.

Grid lines, which are used for this purpose, are shown on these maps. They are the thin lines one kilometre apart drawn vertically and horizontally on the map thus producing a network of small squares. Each line, whether vertical or horizontal, is given a number from 00 to 99, with the sequence repeating itself every 100 lines. The 00 lines are slightly thicker than the others thus producing large squares each side representing 100 km and made up of 100 small squares. Each of these large squares is

identified by a letter. The entire network of lines covering the island of Ireland is called the National Grid.

The left-hand diagram shows a corner of a map which contains a Youth Hostel. Using this map, the method of determing a grid reference is as follows:

Step 1
Holding the map in the normal upright position, note the number of the 'vertical' grid line to the left of the hostel. This is 72.

Step 2
Now imagine that the space between this grid line and the adjacent one to the right of the hostel is divided into ten equal divisions (the right-hand diagram does this for you). Estimate the number of these 'tenths' that the hostel lies to the right of the left-hand grid line. This is 8. Add this to the number found in Step 1 to make 728.

Step 3
Note the number of the grid line below the hostel and add it on to the number obtained above. This is 21, so that the number becomes 72821.

Step 4
Repeat Step 2 for the space containing the hostel, but now in a vertical direction. The final number to be added is 5, making 728215. This is called a six-figure grid reference. This will enable the Youth Hostel to be found on *any* map on which the National Grid is drawn.

A full grid reference will also include the identification of the appropriate 100 kilometre square of the National Grid; for example, R728215. This information is given on each map.

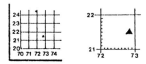

MAPS FOR THE WALKER

The present position on maps for walkers is quite complicated. Because the recommended map or maps is given for each walk within the text, it is more appropriate here to concentrate on the advantages and disadvantages of the various series and to give the coverage, which is patchy and in any case changing rapidly, only in very general terms.

125

Northern Ireland

A good 1:50 000 layer-tinted series with 10 m contour intervals covers the entire area and a few neighbouring parts of the Republic. It shows paths, forests and cliffs accurately, and although the colouring is in places laid on with a heavy hand so that it can be difficult to read contours on the hills, these maps are generally excellent.

A 1:25 000 map covers the Mournes; it is in the same series as the excellent British series. One disadvantage of this map is that its large size makes it hardly suitable for refolding in high winds on a mountainside, which its large scale makes necessary frequently.

The other relevant Northern Ireland series is the half-inch to the mile (1:126 720), which is useful not because of its coverage of Northern Ireland, but because it covers some areas of the north of the Republic not covered so well by the Republic's maps.

The Republic

The whole state is covered by a half-inch to the mile (1:126 720) series with 100 ft contour intervals. The series is none too accurate: forests are vaguely indicated; roads and paths tend to be out of date; and cliffs are indicated, but are so patchy and inaccurate that the symbols are of limited value. Where there is a choice, the half-inch Northern series should be used as it is much superior, not least in presentation. It is hardly necessary to add that the scale is far too small. For instance, to represent the 48 sq miles (12,500 hectares) of the complex tangle of peaks, ridges and valleys of the Twelve Bens on a baggage-label-sized 12 sq in (80 sq cm) is clearly grossly inadequate.

Four areas, three of which are of interest to walkers, are covered by the 'District' one-inch to the mile (1:63 360) series. The maps in this series are layer-tinted and have a 100 ft contour interval to 1000 ft and 250 ft above 1000 ft – hence they give the impression that Irish mountains are gently sloped in their higher reaches. Paths are shown except for the very significant omission of the Long Distance Routes. Perhaps it might be more accurate to say that they are shown as they were 100 years ago. Cliffs are badly and inaccurately depicted. Forests are clearly depicted but are not always up to date; inexplicably, forest tracks are usually highly inaccurate. In general this series is barely

adequate, and the contouring in particular is poor. It should also be noted that only a small proportion of the mountain area is covered.

The latest series to appear, called the Discovery Series, is by far the best. This series is totally metric, with a scale of 1:50 000. The earlier sheets in the series are not layer-tinted, the later (and better) ones are. Cliffs are not explicitly depicted and have to be judged by the convergence of contour lines, though the lines have inexplicably been omitted for some sea-cliffs. Paths are not adequately shown (except some Long Distance Routes) and the depiction of forests is poor, but these are comparatively minor matters. This series is recommended for the areas it covers – these now comprise most of the mountain areas in the State. The Ordnance Survey hope to cover the entire area of the State at 1:50 000 by 1998–1999.

Finally, one special-purpose series and one privately produced map should be mentioned; other maps of specific areas are covered as they occur in the walk descriptions. The special-purpose series is that published by the Office of Public Works and is available at National Park centres. The series covers the small National Parks and surrounding areas on a scale of one-inch to the mile (1:63 360) with 100 ft contour intervals, and with cliffs roughly indicated (one of the series, Glendalough is at 1:25 000 with a 15 m contour interval). The series is quite reliable and up to date. The paper is flimsy, but since the maps cost only a few pence each this does not matter too much, unless the map disintegrates in pouring rain on an unknown mountainside – as tends to happen.

A private firm, Folding Landscapes, Round-stone, Co. Galway, has published a map (and guide) to Connemara on a scale of 1:50 000 with a 30 m contour interval and cliffs accurately depicted. Unfortunately, the paper is very flimsy. However, the map shows paths, forests and placenames accurately and comprehensively. Placenames are shown in the original Gaelic form, not the anglicized versions recorded by surveyors in the last century.

For the walks covered by the Connemara map this has led to a problem: whether to use the mangled but well-known anglicized versions or the 'correct' but little-known Gaelic ones. Both versions are given at the first mention and thereafter the anglicized.

ADDRESSES OF USEFUL ORGANIZATIONS

Republic of Ireland

An Oige – Youth Hostel Association of Ireland
61 Mountjoy Street, Dublin 7
Tel: (01) 830 4555

An Taisce – National Trust for Ireland
Tailors Hall, Back Lane,
Dublin 8
Tel: (01) 454 4794

Association for Adventure Sports
House of Sport, Longmile Road,
Dublin 12
Tel: (01) 450 9845

Bord Failte Eireann – Irish Tourist Board
Baggot Street Bridge, Dublin 2
Tel: (01) 676 5871

Coillte Teoranta – Irish Forestry Board
Leeson Lane, Dublin 2
Tel: (01) 615 666

Conservation Volunteers Ireland
Royal Dublin Society, Dublin 4
Tel: (01) 681 228

Cospoir – The National Sports Council
Hawkins House, Hawkins Street,
Dublin 2
Tel: (01) 873 4700
(*responsible for Long Distance Routes*)

Irish Peatland Conservation Council
119 Capel Street, Dublin 1
Tel: (01) 872 2397

Irish Wildbird Conservancy
Ruttledge House, 8 Longford Place,
Monkstown, Co Dublin
Tel: (01) 280 4322

Irish Wildlife Federation
132a East Wall Road, Dublin 3
Tel: (01) 836 6821

Mountaineering Council of Ireland
House of Sport, Longmile Road,
Dublin 12
Tel: (01) 450 9845

Office of Public Works
51 St Stephens Green, Dublin 2
Tel: (01) 661 3111
(*OPW is responsible for National Parks*)

Ordnance Survey of Ireland
Phoenix Park, Dublin 8
Tel: (01) 820 6100

Northern Ireland

Conservation Volunteers (Northern Ireland)
The Pavilion,
Cherryfield Playing Fields,
Ravenhill Road, Belfast, BT6 0BZ
Tel: (01232) 645 169

Department of the Environment
Conservation Service
Calvert House, 23 Castle Place,
Belfast, BT1 1FY
Tel: (01232) 230 560

National Trust
Regional Office, Rowallane House,
Saintfield, BT24 7LH
Tel: (01238) 510 721

Northern Ireland Tourist Board
River House, 48 High Street,
Belfast, BT1 2DS
Tel: (01232) 246 609

Ordnance Survey of Northern Ireland
Colby House, Stranmillis,
Belfast, BT9 5BJ
Tel: (01232) 661 244

Royal Society for the Protection of Birds
Belvoir Forest, Belvoir Park,
Belfast, BT8 4QT
Tel: (01232) 491 547

Sports Council for Northern Ireland
House of Sport, Upper Malone Road,
Belfast, BT9 5LA
Tel: (01232) 381 222
(*Responsible for Long Distance Routes*)

Youth Hostel Association of Northern Ireland
56 Bradbury Place, Belfast, BT7 1RU
Tel: (01232) 324 733

INDEX